The Polarized Public?

Why American Government Is So Dysfunctional

The Polarized Public?

Why American Government Is So Dysfunctional

ALAN I. ABRAMOWITZ

EMORY UNIVERSITY

PEARSON

Boston   Columbus   Indianapolis   New York   San Francisco   Upper Saddle River
Amsterdam   Cape Town   Dubai   London   Madrid   Milan   Munich   Paris   Montreal   Toronto
Delhi   Mexico City   São Paulo   Sydney   Hong Kong   Seoul   Singapore   Taipei   Tokyo

Executive Editor: Reid Hester
Executive Marketing Manager: Wendy Gordon
Production/Project Manager: Laura Messerly
Senior Art Director: Jayne Conte
Cover Designer: Bruce Kenselaar
Cover Art: Dreamstime
Full-service Project Management: Chitra Sundarajan/PreMediaGlobal
Composition: PreMediaGlobal
Printer/Binder: R.R. Donnelley/Harrisonburg
Cover Printer: R.R. Donnelley/Harrisonburg

Credits and acknowledgments for material borrowed from other sources and reproduced, with permission, in this textbook appear on the appropriate page within text.

Library of Congress Cataloging-in-Publication Data
Abramowitz, Alan.
  The polarized public: why our government is so dysfunctional / Alan I. Abramowitz.
    p. cm.
  Includes index.
  ISBN-13: 978-0-205-87739-3 (alk. paper)
  ISBN-10: 0-205-87739-7 (alk. paper)
1. Political parties—United States—History—21st century.   2. Party affiliation—United States—History—21st century.   3. Polarization (Social sciences)—United States—History—21st century.
4. Ideology—United States—History—21st century.   5. Elections—United States—History—21st century.   6. Two-party systems—United States.   7. Divided government—United States—History—21st century.   8. United States—Politics and government—21st century.   I. Title.
  JK2271.A37 2013
  320.50973—dc23
                                                                        2011048323

10 9 8 7 6 5 4 3 2 1

ISBN 10: 0-205-87739-7
ISBN 13: 978-0-205-87739-3

To those who care enough about America
to choose sides

Politics Ain't Beanbag.
Finley Peter Dunne

Contents

CHAPTER 7

Preface

We have met the enemy, and he is us.

—Pogo

Americans love to complain about their government and political leaders. It's a tradition as old as our democracy. And lately, it does seem that there is a lot to complain about. The nation faces grave challenges at home and abroad, from stubbornly high unemployment and a soaring budget deficit to global warming and unfinished wars in Iraq and Afghanistan. Yet our elected leaders seem incapable of responding effectively to these problems. Instead, they seem to be caught up in an endless game of gotcha—Democrats blaming Republicans and Republicans blaming Democrats.

The natural tendency, under these circumstances, is to blame the politicians themselves for their inability to bridge the partisan divide in Washington and come up with solutions to the country's problems. Indeed, this approach plays into the populist sentiments of the American public. Ordinary Americans, according to this line of reasoning, are blameless for the polarization and gridlock in Washington. They are innocent victims of the machinations of the Washington political elite and a small band of ideologically extreme activists who abhor compromise. In the words of Morris Fiorina and his coauthors, "most Americans are somewhat like the unfortunate citizens of some third-world countries who try to stay out of the crossfire while left-wing guerrillas and right-wing death squads shoot at each other."[1]

---

[1] Morris P. Fiorina with Samuel J. Abrams and Jeremy C. Pope, *Culture War? The Myth of a Polarized America*, 3rd ed. (New York: Longman 2011), p. 8.

It is an appealing theory—one that has found considerable favor with pundits and political commentators in recent years. But despite its popularity, the elite theory of polarization is based on a fundamentally flawed understanding of the relationship between political leaders and the American public in the twenty-first century. According to this theory, there is a huge disconnect between the "political class" and the public in the United States. Elected officials hang out at the extremes of the ideological spectrum while the vast majority of the voters who chose them are clustered in the center. However, the theory never really explains why this is the case. Why would senators, members of Congress, state legislators, and even presidents take positions that are so far removed from the preferences of the citizens whose votes put them in office and whose votes they need to stay in office?

The short answer to this question, which will be explained in much greater depth in the chapters that follow, is that they wouldn't. As anyone who has spent any time with these elected officials knows, they are hypersensitive to the views of those citizens whose support they depend on for their positions. But in today's America, Democrats and Republicans depend on the support of citizens with very different views on the major issues facing the country. That is the fundamental fact underlying the deep partisan divide in Washington and in so many of our state capitols today: rank-and-file Democrats and Republicans are themselves deeply divided.

Democrats and Republicans are deeply divided by race, by ideology, by religious beliefs and moral values, and by geography. And the more they care about politics, pay attention to what their elected representatives are doing, and participate in the political process, the more divided they are. Those Americans whose attitudes and behavior most closely reflect the ideals of democratic citizenship are the most partisan and the most polarized. In contrast, it is among the uninterested, uninformed, and uninvolved that moderation and independence flourish.[2]

---

[2]See Alan I. Abramowitz, *The Disappearing Center: Engaged Citizens, Polarization and American Democracy* (New Haven: Yale University Press, 2010).

There is no disconnect between elected officials and the voters who put them in office; there is, in fact, a close connection between them. Polarization is not a result of a failure of representation; it is a result of successful representation. Democrats and Republicans in Washington and in our state capitols are accurately reflecting the divergent views of their supporters, and especially their politically engaged supporters. If concerned citizens want to understand the root cause of polarization and government gridlock, they should heed the words of Pogo and look in a mirror.

THE PLAN OF THIS BOOK

The remainder of this book will examine the causes and consequences of polarization in the American public. In Chapter 1, we will focus on one of the most divisive policy issues that our country has dealt with in recent years—health care reform. Few issues, if any, have produced such a sharp partisan divide in Congress: Democrats overwhelmingly support efforts to expand the role of the federal government in regulating the health care system in order to provide health insurance to millions of Americans and Republicans unanimously oppose these efforts. Even after the Affordable Care Act was passed by Congress on a nearly straight party line vote and signed into law by President Obama, the battle continued with the new Republican majority in the House of Representatives voting to repeal "ObamaCare" as one of its first acts in 2011. We will see that the key to understanding the deep divisions in Washington over health care reform is the deep divisions that exist between rank-and-file Democrats and Republicans in the public. On this issue, as on many others, polarization in Washington reflects polarization in the country.

Chapter 2 will examine what may be the most important long-term trend contributing to the rise of polarization in twenty-first century America—the steady increase in the racial and ethnic diversity of the American population. In the 16 years between 1992 and 2008, the nonwhite share of the U.S. electorate doubled, from 13 to 26 percent. And this trend is almost certain to continue for the foreseeable future. In 2007, according to data from the U.S. Census Bureau, nonwhites made up almost half of the U.S. population under the age of 5 compared with less than 10 percent of the population over the age of seventy. Latinos make up about a quarter of the under-age-5 population compared with less than 5 percent of the over-age-70 population. So even if immigration to the United States from Mexico and other parts of Latin America slows, the nonwhite, and especially the Latino, share of the population and the electorate will continue to grow. In fact, Census Bureau projections indicate that by 2050, the United States will be a majority-minority country.

The growing racial and ethnic diversity of the electorate has had major consequences for American politics. The movement of nonwhite voters into the Democratic Party and the corresponding movement of conservative white voters out of the Democratic Party and into the Republican Party have transformed both parties' electoral coalitions and thereby contributed to ideological polarization. Today the Democratic electoral coalition is dominated by nonwhites and white liberals who strongly support activist government; the Republican electoral coalition is dominated by white conservatives who strongly oppose activist government, especially activist government that is seen as primarily benefiting nonwhites.

There is no reason to believe that these trends will stop or be reversed any time soon. In fact, data from the 2008 national exit poll indicate that the racial divide between the two parties was greatest among the youngest voters and census data indicate that the nonwhite share of the U.S. population will continue to increase for the next several decades. Based on these results, we can expect the racial and ethnic divide between the party coalitions to continue to grow for the foreseeable future.

Chapter 3 will focus on the ideological realignment of the American party system over the past fifty years. The second major force underlying polarization, along with the demographic transformation of the U.S. population, has been this ideological realignment. During the 1960s and 1970s, as the national Democratic Party embraced the cause of civil rights and the Republican Party began aggressively courting racially and culturally conservative whites in the South and elsewhere, African-Americans went from being a solidly Democratic voting bloc to being an overwhelmingly Democratic voting bloc. Meanwhile, within the white electorate, those with conservative views on racial and cultural issues, such as men, married voters, and frequent churchgoers, shifted their loyalties to the Republicans while those with more liberal views on these issues, such as women, single voters, and infrequent churchgoers, continued to support the Democrats.

The end result of all of these changes has been the emergence of a new American party system—one in which party loyalties are based primarily on voters' ideological beliefs rather than their membership in social groups. Moreover, the ideological divide between party support-ers is greatest among those who are the most interested, informed, and politically active—a group that has actually been growing in size in recent years. Among the engaged public, the group whose views candidates and elected officials are most concerned with, there is now a very deep ideo-logical divide between the parties.

Fiorina and his coauthors have acknowledged that Americans today are better sorted by party than in the past—that is, there is a closer alignment of party and ideology—but they deny that we are any more polarized than we were in the 1950s and 1960s. I will present evidence that this is not the case, however. In fact, both sorting, a growing divide between Democratic and Republican identifiers, and polarization, a more divided distribution of ideological views, have been increas-ing and these two trends are very closely related. Sorting by party is actually an important contributor to growing ideological polarization among the public and especially among the politically engaged segment of the public.

An important and underestimated factor in growing polarization among the politically engaged segment of the public is the growing con-sistency of opinions across issues. This means that rather than agreeing with the Democratic position on some issues and the Republican position on other issues, politically engaged citizens increasingly find themselves agreeing with one party and disagreeing with the opposing party on issue after issue. Not only does this growing consistency lead to stronger party loyalties and increased party-line voting, but it may also contribute to a tendency to demonize the opposing party and its supporters.

Chapter 4 will focus on the impact of cultural issues on polarization in recent years. The growing importance of issues such as abortion and gay marriage in American politics in recent decades has contributed to a deepening of the ideological divide between the Democratic and Republican parties. While traditional economic issues continue to divide the parties, cultural issues are often more divisive than economic issues because they reflect deeply held religious beliefs and moral values. Moreover, these issues increasingly reinforce each other—the most politically engaged partisans now tend to hold consistent views on economic and cultural issues. As a result, differences on economic issues often become infused with moral significance. Those on the opposing side are viewed not only as wrong but as immoral and un-American. Cultural issues have played a major role in both the rise of the religious right during the 1970s and 1980s and the more recent emergence of the Tea Party movement following the 2008 election.

Chapter 5 will examine geographic polarization in the United States. Demographic trends and ideological realignment have produced dramatic changes over the past several decades in the patterns of geographic support for the two major parties. The South, once the stronghold of the Democratic Party, has been transformed into the most Republican region of the nation while the Northeast, which was once a bastion of Republican support, has emerged as the most Democratic region. Along with this reversal in the traditional geographic bases of the parties, there has also been a growing divide between Democratic and Republican regions of the country. Over the past several decades, the number of marginal House districts has been declining while the number of safe Democratic and Republican districts has been growing, and this trend cannot be explained by partisan gerrymandering. The same trend is evident at the state level—there are fewer battleground states and more landslide states than in the past.

This trend toward more and more "deep red and blue" districts and states is a result of both population shifts and ideological realignment. Americans have been choosing where to locate based in part on lifestyle preferences that are associated with political outlook. In addition, areas with growing minority populations have generally been trending Democratic while areas with more conservative white populations have been trending Republican. These shifts have had important consequences for elections and representation. Despite the relatively even balance between the parties in the nation, more and more Democratic and Republican elected officials now represent constituencies dominated by their own party. For these elected officials, there is little need to appeal to supporters of the opposing party or to swing voters. In fact, for many elected officials today, the primary election is a more significant concern than the general election.

Chapter 6 will examine one of the most important consequences of growing polarization within the American electorate in recent years—the rise of the Tea Party movement following the 2008 election. At the grassroots level, the emergence of the Tea Party movement can best be understood as an outgrowth of the increased conservatism of the Republican electoral base, and especially the more politically engaged segment of that base, since the 1970s. I present evidence from American National Election Study (ANES) surveys showing that Republican identifiers have been trending in a conservative direction for several decades and that this trend has been most evident among the most active partisans. I then present evidence from the October 2010 wave of the ANES Evaluations of Government and Society Survey about the social characteristics and political beliefs of Tea Party supporters.

The overwhelming majority of Tea Party supporters in 2010 were Republicans and supporters were much more conservative than other Republicans. While conservatism is by far the strongest predictor of support for the Tea Party movement, racial hostility also has a significant impact on support. Along with their greater conservatism, Tea Party supporters were much more politically active than other Republicans. These results suggest that the Tea Party movement has the potential to strongly influence the 2012 Republican congressional and presidential primaries, putting considerable pressure on Republican candidates to embrace issue positions well to the right of the median general election voter.

Chapter 7, the concluding chapter of the book, will examine the outlook for the 2012 election and beyond in light of the consequences of the long-term trends discussed in the book and the results of the 2008 and 2010 elections. I will argue that both Barack Obama's stunning victory in 2008 and the Republican comeback in 2010 can be understood as results of the increasing polarization of American politics and that this trend is likely to continue in 2012. The growing demographic and ideological divides evident in the 2008 and 2010 results and the emergence of the Tea Party movement as a major force within the Republican Party almost guarantee that the Republican presidential nominee in 2012 will present voters with a sharp ideological contrast with President Obama. In the congressional elections as well, the few remaining moderate Republicans and even some mainstream conservatives may face strong challenges from Tea Party–backed candidates. The result should be a divisive but exciting campaign that will probably produce a high level of public engagement and voter turnout. However, given the close division between the two major parties in the country, the chances that the presidential and congressional elections will produce a decisive enough result to overcome gridlock and dysfunctional government appear to be slim.

From the standpoint of effective governance, a key question is how the growing ideological divide among political elites and the engaged segment of the public interacts with political institutions that can make it difficult for either party to carry out its policy commitments. Despite the nostalgia of some political commentators for a lost era of bipartisan consensus, the traditional bipartisan approach, in which public policy is based on compromise between key leaders in both major parties, now appears to be almost dead. The differences between the parties are too great and the numbers of moderates in both parties are too small to permit such bipartisan agreements on major policy issues. Political leaders today find themselves trapped by the polarized preferences of their politically engaged supporters.

The question is, what will replace the politics of bipartisan compromise? I will argue that the only realistic alternative to continued gridlock in Washington is not a revival of bipartisanship but an American version of responsible party government. However, I will also argue that responsible party government cannot work without some fundamental reforms, especially ending the filibuster in the Senate. The combination of a political system incorporating antimajoritarian institutions and rules with an increasingly polarized party system is almost guaranteed to produce dysfunctional government and gridlock.

Acknowledgments

I owe a debt of gratitude to many individuals whose ideas have contributed to my thinking about polarization and American democracy, including my undergraduate and graduate students at Emory University. I have benefited greatly from my collaboration with Kyle Saunders of Colorado State University, Ronald Rapoport of the College of William and Mary, Walter Stone of the University of California at Davis, and Ruy Teixeira of the Center for American Progress. Larry Sabato of the Center for Politics at the University of Virginia and Bill Bishop of the *Austin American-Statesman* have influenced my thinking about recent trends in American society and politics. And I am grateful to Jim Campbell of the State University of New York at Buffalo for providing a useful perspective on polarization from the other side of the partisan and ideological divide. I have also learned much from my colleagues at Emory University, including Merle Black, Randall Strahan, Thomas Remington, and Micheal Giles. I would also like to thank Reid Hester, Political Science Editor at Pearson Longman, for his encouragement of this project. I am especially grateful to George C. Edwards III of Texas A&M University, the editor of the *Great Questions in Politics* series, for his encouragement and for his very helpful comments and suggestions on each of the chapters in this book. Finally, I would like to thank my wife, Ann, for her encouragement and support on this project, for keeping my ideas firmly grounded in the real political world and for always letting me know when I have got it wrong.

CHAPTER I

The Polarized Public

This legislation will lead to healthier lives, more liberty to pursue hopes and dreams and happiness for the American people. This is an American proposal that honors the traditions of our country.
—House Speaker Nancy Pelosi (D-CA), March 21, 2010

This is a government takeover of our healthcare system. It is the government basically running the entire healthcare system, turning large insurers into de facto public utilities, depriving people of choice, depriving people of options, raising people's prices, raising taxes when we need new jobs.
—U.S. Representative Paul Ryan (R-WI), March 22, 2010

Perhaps no issue has produced greater controversy and deeper partisan division in recent years than health care reform. The Patient Protection and Affordable Care Act signed into law by President Obama on March 23, 2010, was enacted over the opposition of every Republican member of the Senate and House of Representatives. Indeed, Republican leaders made repeal of the law their top legislative priority after their party regained control of the House of Representatives in the 2010 midterm elections. On January 19, 2011, all 242 House Republicans voted for the repeal legislation while 186 of 189 House Democrats voted against repeal. Less than two weeks later, the Democratic-controlled Senate rejected the repeal legislation on a straight party-line vote. Nevertheless, Republican leaders vowed to continue their efforts to block implementation of the law and promised to make health care reform, or as they preferred to call it, ObamaCare, a major issue in the 2012 elections.[1]

While the debate over health care reform has been particularly contentious, the deep partisan divide on this issue is far from unique. Over the past forty years, the gap between the two parties in Congress has steadily widened across a wide range of policy issues. According to a statistical analysis of voting patterns in the House and Senate, since the 1960s, the Republican Party has moved sharply to the right while the Democratic Party has moved, if not quite as dramatically, to the left. Liberal Republicans and conservative Democrats who exercised considerable influence in their respective parties during the 1950s and 1960s are now almost extinct.[2]

In 2010, the most recent year for which data were available, the ideological gap between the average Democrat and the average Republican in both chambers was greater than at any time in the previous hundred years. However, the gap may be even larger in the Congress that took office in 2011. Most of the Democrats who lost their seats in the 2010 midterm election were moderates representing swing states and districts but their replacements were generally very conservative Republicans, many elected with the support of the Tea Party movement. In fact, the House Republicans elected in 2010 appear to be considerably more conservative as a group than those who served in the House under Newt Gingrich in 1995–96. They may well be the most conservative group of House Republicans since the end of World War II.[3] Meanwhile, with the loss of many of their moderate members, the remaining House Democrats were considerably more liberal than those serving in the previous Congress.

---

[1]For an excellent overview of the debate over health care reform, see Lawrence R. Jacobs and Theda Skocpol, *Health Care Reform and American Politics: What Everyone Needs to Know* (New York: Oxford University Press, 2010). See also, Washington Post Staff, *Landmark: The Inside Story of America's New Health Care Law and What It Means for Us All* (Washington, DC: Public Affairs Books, 2010).

[2]These trends are summarized in graphic form at http://www.voteview.com/dwnomin_joint_house_and_senate.htm. For an in-depth analysis of trends in polarization in Congress, see Keith T. Poole and Howard Rosenthal, *Ideology and Congress* (New York: Transaction Books, 2009).

[3]Alan I. Abramowitz, "Expect Confrontation, Not Compromise: The 112th House of Representatives Is Likely to Be the Most Conservative and Polarized House in the Modern Era," *PS: Political Science and Politics* 44 (April 2011): 293–96.

And while the changes in the makeup of the Senate were not as dramatic as those in the House, the divide between the two parties in the upper chamber appeared to be at least as great as that in the previous Congress, as indicated by the straight party-line vote on repeal of health care reform.

Polarization in recent years has by no means been limited to the House of Representatives and Senate. There have also been sharp differences between the party nominees for president on a wide range of policy issues, including health care, taxes, financial regulation, abortion, stem cell research, gay rights, and the war in Iraq. And while these differences were perhaps most accentuated during the nomination campaigns, when the candidates were appealing to their parties' primary voters, they were clearly visible during the fall general election campaigns as well. There was little evidence, for example, that either Barack Obama or John McCain tried to move toward the center after winning their party's nominations in 2008. In fact, McCain's most important decision after securing the Republican nomination was to choose Alaska Governor Sarah Palin as his running mate—a decision clearly aimed at energizing his party's conservative base rather than appealing to moderate swing voters.[4]

Regardless of who wins the 2012 Republican presidential nomination, it is certain that the general election campaign will present voters with a clear choice between candidates offering widely diverging policies for addressing the challenges facing the country. As president, Mr. Obama, while hardly the radical socialist regularly castigated by right-wing talk show hosts and Republican leaders, has advanced an activist agenda, including, in addition to health care reform, an $800 billion economic stimulus package, stricter environmental regulations including regulation of greenhouse gases, tougher rules governing major financial institutions, increased federal aid to education, and repeal of the controversial "don't ask, don't tell" policy restricting the ability of gays and lesbians to serve openly in the U.S. military. Meanwhile, every one of the leading Republican presidential candidates, in addition to opposing all of these initiatives, has

[4]See John Heilemann and Mark Halperin, *Game Change: Obama and the Clintons, McCain and Palin, and the Race of a Lifetime* (New York: Harper, 2010).

endorsed a budget plan proposed by Wisconsin Representative Paul Ryan, who envisions drastic cuts in domestic spending, elimination of capital gains and estate taxes, and replacing traditional Medicare with vouchers requiring senior citizens to purchase health care plans from private insurance companies.[5] The Ryan Medicare plan, in particular, proved to be highly controversial, with several polls showing strong public opposition. However, when one Republican presidential candidate, former House Speaker Newt Gingrich, dared to question the advisability of the proposed Medicare changes, he was sharply attacked by conservative pundits and politicians and forced to take back his comments.[6]

Growing polarization has also been evident in recent years at the state level. Traditionally, political parties in the United Sates have been highly decentralized, with Democratic and Republican state parties often taking positions on major issues at variance with those of their national counterparts. Democratic state parties in the South were typically much more conservative than the national Democratic Party, and Republican state parties in the Northeast were generally much more liberal than the national Republican Party. While there is still some ideological variation among Democratic and Republican state parties, the differences are generally much smaller than in the past.

Today, the ideological divide between the parties in the states is very similar to the ideological divide between the national parties. In fact, since the 2010 elections, some of the sharpest ideological confrontations between the parties have been taking place at the state level as newly elected conservative Republican governors and state legislative majorities have sought to implement controversial policies, including sharp cuts in spending on social programs and curbs on the benefits and bargaining rights of public employees. In states from Wisconsin to Florida and Michigan to New Jersey, public employees and their Democratic allies

---

[5]David Catanese, "Paul Ryan Budget Becomes Litmus Test for GOP Primaries," *Politico* (June 23, 2011): http://www.politico.com/news/stories/0611/57678.html.

[6]See Mara Liasson, "Gingrich Backpedals on Medicare Comments in Iowa," National Public Radio, May 20, 2011: http://www.npr.org/2011/05/20/136467767/gingrich-backpedals-medicare-comments-in-iowa.

have fought back against legislation proposed by conservative Republicans with actions ranging from walkouts and mass demonstrations to recall elections.[7] In Minnesota, a confrontation between the Democratic governor and the Republican state legislature over the state budget resulted in a partial government shutdown reminiscent of the one that affected the federal government during the 1990s.[8]

THE DEBATE: ELITE VERSUS MASS POLARIZATION

There is general agreement among political scientists and other observers of American politics that partisan polarization has substantially increased among political leaders and activists over the past several decades. Almost everyone agrees that Democratic and Republican elites—public officials, candidates, party leaders, and campaign activists—are much more sharply divided along ideological lines today than at any time in the recent past. It might be necessary to go back to the years immediately preceding the Civil War to find a time when the two major parties were as polarized as they are today. However, there is considerable disagreement about whether and to what extent polarization has also increased among the large majority of Americans who are not deeply involved in the political process—the mass public.

According to one school of thought, represented most prominently by political scientist Morris Fiorina and his coauthors, polarization in the United States is almost exclusively an elite phenomenon. They have forcefully argued that among the vast majority of Americans who are not actively involved in politics, polarization has not increased.[9] In their

---

[7]Probably no state's budget battle has received more national publicity than Wisconsin's. See Tom Tolan, "First Round in Senate Recall Elections Draws Near," *Milwaukee Journal-Sentinel* (July 2, 2011): http://www.jsonline.com/news/statepolitics/124925369.html.

[8]James Hohmann, "Minnesota Mean at Heart of Government Shutdown," *Politico* (July 3, 2011): http://www.politico.com/news/stories/0711/58260.html.

[9]Morris P. Fiorina, with Samuel J. Abrams and Jeremy C. Pope, *Culture War? The Myth of a Polarized America*, 3rd ed. (New York: Longman, 2011). See also Morris P. Fiorina and Matthew S. Levendusky, "Disconnected: The Political Class versus the People," in *Red and Blue Nation? Characteristics and Causes of America's Polarized Politics*, vol. 1, ed. Pietro S. Nivola and David W. Brady (Washington, DC: Brookings Institution, 2006).

view, ordinary Americans today, much like their counterparts forty or fifty years ago, are not very interested in politics and not very informed about the ideological debates that preoccupy officeholders. Moreover, in contrast to members of the political elite, their opinions tend to cluster around the center of the ideological spectrum. Very few ordinary citizens take consistently liberal or conservative positions on major policy issues.

Fiorina and his coauthors claim that there is a growing disconnect in American politics between an increasingly polarized political elite and a largely centrist public.[10] Ordinary citizens, they argue, are turned off by the relatively extreme positions of both parties. As a result, a growing number of Americans consider themselves independents and many prefer to stay at home on Election Day rather than choose between two extreme alternatives. In their words, "Americans are closely divided, but we are not deeply divided, and we are closely divided because many of us are ambivalent and uncertain, and consequently reluctant to make firm commitments to parties, politicians, or policies. We divide evenly in elections or sit them out entirely because we instinctively seek the center while the parties and candidates hang out on the extremes."[11]

The elite theory of polarization has found considerable favor among pundits and political commentators. It is an appealing line of argument because it absolves the large majority of Americans of any responsibility for the dysfunctional condition of our political system. According to this theory, it is the political elites—officeholders, candidates, and a small group of activists—who are to blame for hyper-partisanship and gridlock. The rest of us are merely victims. We are, in effect, trapped in a polarized party system that we had nothing to do with creating.

Despite its appeal, however, the elite theory of polarization suffers from several major shortcomings when subjected to a careful examination of the arguments and the evidence. First, the theory fails to explain why ambitious political leaders would adopt extreme positions that are

---

[10]Morris P. Fiorina with Samuel J. Abrams, *Disconnect: The Breakdown of Representation in American Politics* (Norman: University of Oklahoma Press, 2009).

[11]Fiorina with Abrams and Pope, *Culture War?*, p. xv.

far out of line with the preferences of those who elect them. According to the well-known median voter theorem, in a centrist electorate, politicians seeking to win elections should adopt centrist positions.[12] Taking extreme positions in a centrist electorate would appear to be a recipe for political oblivion, as Barry Goldwater and George McGovern discovered in their disastrous presidential bids. Even if candidates were forced to adopt relatively extreme positions to appeal to their party's primary voters, one would expect them to move back toward the center during the general election campaign. The fact that this does not seem to be happening suggests that the general election voters are themselves more polarized than in the past.

Second, the claim that the political beliefs of the American public have changed little since the 1950s seems rather implausible in light of the dramatic changes that have affected American politics and society over the past six decades. These changes have included an ideological and regional realignment of the two-party system that has resulted in much clearer differences between the ideological positions of Democratic and Republican officeholders and candidates, rising levels of education within the public, the changing structure of the mass media, the increasing salience of cultural issues, and growing racial and ethnic diversity. It is hard to believe that these sweeping changes have had no impact on the way ordinary Americans think about politics. We will see in the chapters that follow that there have in fact been substantial changes in Americans' political attitudes over the past half century.

Finally, and perhaps most importantly, broad generalizations about the low level of ideological sophistication of the American public ignore the enormous diversity that exists within the public with regard to political engagement. While many Americans have little or no interest in politics, ignore news about government and politics, and rarely vote or participate in politics in any way, many others care a great deal about politics, follow news about government and politics closely, vote regularly, talk about politics with their friends and neighbors, and donate time and money

---

[12]This theory is most famously explained in Anthony Downs, *An Economic Theory of Democracy* (New York: Harper & Row, 1957), chapter 8.

to candidates and political parties. Few Americans are political junkies whose lives revolve around politics but few are totally apolitical.

Political engagement varies widely within the American public, and we will see that this fact goes a long way toward explaining polarization among political elites. That is because political engagement is strongly related to polarization. The more engaged Americans are in the political process—the more they care about politics, the more they know about politics, and the more they participate in politics—the more partisan and the more polarized they tend to be. In the twenty-first century, the ideals of democratic citizenship are best exemplified by those Americans with the strongest partisan and ideological convictions. In contrast, it is among the uninterested, the uninformed, and the uninvolved that political independence and moderation flourish.[13]

Contrary to the claims made by Fiorina and his coauthors, there is no disconnect between political elites and the public. Instead, the evidence presented in this book shows that political elites represent the views of the politically engaged segment of the public. Moreover, the politically engaged segment of the public has been growing in size in response to the increasing polarization of the parties. Voter turnout has been increasing since 1996. In 2008, turnout was higher than in any presidential election since the franchise was extended to 18–20-year-olds in 1972.

And it wasn't just voting that increased in 2004 and 2008. According to data from the American National Election Studies (ANES), in both 2004 and 2008, the percentage of Americans who cared a great deal about the outcome of the election, displayed a yard sign or bumper sticker, and tried to persuade a friend or neighbor to support a candidate was higher than at any time since the beginning of the ANES surveys in 1952. Rather than being turned off by polarization, as Fiorina and his coauthors have claimed, Americans actually have been energized by a choice between party nominees taking sharply contrasting policy positions.[14]

---

[13]For an extended analysis of the role of the engaged public in polarization, see Alan I. Abramowitz, *The Disappearing Center: Engaged Citizens, Polarization and American Democracy* (New Haven: Yale University Press, 2010).

[14]Abramowitz, *The Disappearing Center*, chapter 2.

EVIDENCE FOR MASS POLARIZATION: THE CASE OF HEALTH CARE REFORM

If polarization among political leaders reflects polarization among the politically engaged segment of the American public, we cannot simply blame hyper-partisanship and gridlock in government on a small unrepresentative political elite. The ultimate source of these problems is found among those members of the public who exemplify the ideals of democratic citizenship—those who pay attention to politics and who care about political issues. And nowhere is this relationship between political elites and politically engaged citizens better illustrated than on the issue with which we began our discussion of polarization—health care reform.

Throughout 2009 and early 2010, as the House of Representatives and Senate were debating the issue of health care reform, demonstrations opposing the Democratic health care reform bill were taking place in cities across the country. At the same time, many Democratic members of Congress found themselves confronted at town hall meetings by concerned and sometimes angry constituents who wanted to express their opposition to the health care bill. Many of the antireform activities were organized by groups aligned with the ultra-conservative Tea Party movement and were actively promoted by Fox News Network. Meanwhile, liberal groups sought to organize counterdemonstrations and letter-writing campaigns supporting health care reform.

Only a small minority of Americans, probably no more than 2 or 3 percent, participated in any of the pro- or antireform activities, including the Tea Party demonstrations.[15] However, evidence from public opinion surveys shows that the roots of the intense partisan divisions seen on the issue of health care reform during 2009 and 2010 could be found in the attitudes of a much larger group of Americans who voted and who

---

[15]For an analysis of the rise of the Tea Party movement during 2009 and its impact on the Republican Party, see Vanessa Williamson, Theda Skocpol, and John Coggin, "The Tea Party and the Remaking of Republican Conservatism," *Perspectives on Politics* 9 (March 2011), 25–44. See also Alan Abramowitz, "Grand Old Tea Party: Partisan Polarization and the Rise of the Tea Party Movement." Paper prepared for delivery at the Annual Meeting of the American Political Science Association, Seattle, WA, September 1–4, 2011.

cared about the issue of health care. Among this very large segment of the public, opinions on health care reform were also highly polarized.

The 2008 American National Election Study survey included a question asking respondents to place themselves on a seven-point scale measuring opinions about the creation of a health care system in the United States in which the federal government would pay for all health care costs— a single-payer health care system like Medicare covering all American citizens. Of course, this would have involved a much more radical reform than the actual health care legislation that was ultimately passed by Congress and signed into law by President Obama. The Patient Protection and Affordable Care Act did not even include a "public option" as an alternative for Americans who did not have health insurance through their employers. Nevertheless, the results indicated that there was strong support for a single-payer system: 51 percent of respondents placed themselves on the pro-reform side of the universal health care scale while only 37 percent placed themselves on the antireform side.

In terms of polarization, what is most important about the results of the universal health care question, however, is the fact that before the 2008 presidential election and well before the debate on health care reform in Congress had begun, the American public was already deeply divided along party lines on this issue and that those who cared the most about the issue were the most deeply divided. Overall, Democratic identifiers and independents leaning toward the Democratic Party favored the creation of a single-payer system by a margin of 71 to 17 percent while Republican identifiers and independents leaning toward the Republican Party opposed the creation of a single-payer system by a margin of 63 to 25 percent. Only 12 percent of both Democrats and Republicans placed themselves in the center on the seven-point scale.

As Figure 1.1 shows (see Chapter 1 color insert), the partisan divide was even greater among the 60 percent of Democratic and Republican voters who considered health care reform a very or extremely important issue in the 2008 presidential election. Among these engaged citizens, a group constituting almost half of the entire public, Democrats and Democratic-leaning independents favored reform by a margin of 81 to 14 percent while

FIGURE 1.1

Opinions of Concerned Democratic and Republican Voters on Universal Health Care.

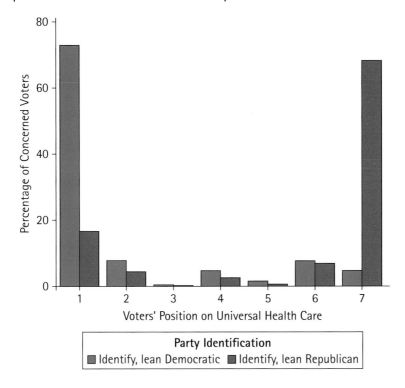

1. Favor a great deal 2. Favor moderately 3. Favor a little 4. Neither favor nor oppose
5. Oppose a little 6. Oppose moderately 7. Oppose a great deal

Source: 2008 American National Election Study

Republicans and Republican-leaning independents favored reform by a margin of 76 to 21 percent. Only 5 percent of concerned Democratic voters and only 3 percent of concerned Republican voters placed themselves in the center on the scale. Almost three-fourths of interested Democratic voters and more than 60 percent of interested Republican voters placed themselves at the polar positions on the scale—strongly supporting reform or strongly opposing reform.

These results show very clearly that before the health care debate in Congress began, before the public demonstrations, and before the raucous town hall meetings, the American people, and especially those who voted on and cared about health care reform, were deeply divided on this issue. The large majority of concerned Democratic voters strongly favored an expanded role for the federal government in providing access to health care while the large majority of concerned Republican voters strongly opposed any such increased federal role. Very few voters who cared about this issue took a moderate position.

Given the opinions of their parties' concerned voters, it is hardly surprising that the debate over health care reform produced a deep and bitter partisan divide in the Congress, with Democrats overwhelmingly supporting an expanded federal role and Republicans unanimously opposing an expanded federal role. On the issue of health care reform, arguably the most important policy issue of the past decade, it is very clear that there was no disconnect between the political elite and the public. Democratic and Republican elites were accurately reflecting the policy preferences of their politically engaged constituents. If anything, the bill passed by Congress and signed into law by President Obama did not go as far as most members of the Democratic base would have liked.[16]

Of course, not every issue in recent years has divided Americans like health care reform. Fiorina and other critics of the mass polarization theory like to point out that there are many things Americans agree about.

---

[16]This was also evident in the results of a question on health care reform in the 2010 national exit poll. While over 80 percent of Republican voters favored repeal of the health care law, more than 60 percent of Democratic voters wanted to see the law expanded. Results of the 2010 exit poll can be found at http://www.cnn.com/ELECTION/2010/results/polls/#val=USH00p1.

Most Americans, regardless of party, love their country, believe in democracy, support basic norms of fairness and equality of opportunity, and favor a free market economy. Some issues such as civil rights that deeply divided Americans in the past are no longer controversial. Moreover, on many issues, differences of opinion based on characteristics such as age, gender, education, religious affiliation, and social class are small or nonexistent.[17]

But these observations, while accurate, have little relevance to the current debate over mass polarization. What matters from the standpoint of mass polarization is that the American public, and especially the politically engaged segment of the public, is deeply divided over the same issues that deeply divide political elites today. And while Americans may not be deeply divided by characteristics such as gender, religious affiliation, and social class, they are deeply divided by party and by other characteristics such as race and religiosity that are closely related to their party's position in the twenty-first century. The party divide is the one that matters the most for both elite and mass polarization because it is political parties that contest elections, organize government, and enact public policy.

CONSTRAINT AND POLARIZATION

While the issue of health care reform has been particularly divisive in recent years, it is far from the only issue on which the American public, and especially the politically engaged segment of the American public, is deeply divided. In fact, one of the most important features of American politics today is not just the intensity of the partisan divisions over hot button issues like health care reform but the range of issues on which these divisions exist and the consistency of opinions across these issues. As Philip Converse argued in his pioneering research on mass belief systems, constraint, or consistency in opinions across issues, is a key characteristic of ideological thinking. It is also a key component of polarization because

---

[17]Paul DiMaggio, John Evans, and Bethany Bryson, "Have Americans' Social Attitudes Become More Polarized?" *American Journal of Sociology* 102 (1996), 690–775; see also John Evans, "Have Americans' Attitudes Become More Polarized? An Update," *Social Science Quarterly* 84 (2003), 71–90.

constraint means that opinions on different issues reinforce each other and push citizens as well as leaders in the same partisan direction. Converse found little evidence of such ideological thinking in the American mass public in the 1950s.[18] We will see, however, that the degree of constraint in public opinion on issues has increased considerably since then, especially among the politically engaged segment of the public.

To a much greater extent than in the past, disagreements on different types of issues tend to coincide with and reinforce one another— disagreements on economic issues increasingly coincide with disagreements on cultural issues, and disagreements on both economic issues and cultural issues increasingly coincide with disagreements on national security issues. And all of these policy disagreements increasingly coincide with party identification. This pattern of reinforcing opinions across issues contributes to the intensity of partisan conflict and to a belief among many Americans that those on the other side of the partisan divide are not just mistaken but immoral or evil. And it is hard to compromise with those who are perceived to be immoral or evil.

EXPLAINING THE RISE OF MASS POLARIZATION

How did we get to this point? What happened to transform Converse's 1950s public in which ideological thinking was rare and partisan conflict was muted into the twenty-first-century public in which ideological thinking is much more prevalent and partisan conflict is much more intense?

In the chapters that follow, we will see that a number of changes in American politics and society have contributed to the rise of mass polarization since the 1950s. One of the most important changes in American politics during this period has been the ideological and regional realignment of the American party system. A prominent feature of the American party system during the 1950s and 1960s was

---

[18]Philip E. Converse, "The Nature of Belief Systems in Mass Publics," in *Ideology and Discontent*, ed. David Apter (New York: The Free Press of Glencoe, 1964), 206–61. See also Angus Campbell, Philip E. Converse, Warren E. Miller, and Donald E. Stokes, *The American Voter* (New York: John Wiley & Sons, 1960), chapter 9.

the ideological diversity of the leadership of the two major parties. This ideological diversity was, in turn, closely related to the regional diversity of the party coalitions. The Democratic Party, though leaning toward the liberal side of the ideological spectrum, included a large and influential conservative wing based mainly in the South. The Republican Party, though leaning toward the conservative side of the ideological spectrum, included a large and influential moderate-to-liberal wing based mainly in the Northeast.

Not surprisingly, given the ideological diversity of both parties' leaders, voters often found it difficult to distinguish between the ideological positions of the two parties. When they were asked by interviewers for the American National Election Studies in 1956 what they liked or disliked about the Democratic and Republican parties and presidential candidates, very few of them mentioned the parties' or candidates' ideologies. Instead, the large majority of comments in response to these open-ended questions dealt with the ways in which the parties or candidates benefited particular groups in society or with the nature of the times.[19]

Over the past fifty years, however, the American party system has undergone a gradual ideological realignment. Sensing an opportunity to expand their party's electoral coalition, Republican leaders beginning with Richard Nixon assiduously courted the support of traditional conservative Democrats in the South and elsewhere who were upset about their party's embrace of civil rights and other liberal causes.[20] They were largely successful and later were able to expand the Republican base to include religious conservatives opposed to legalized abortion, bans on school prayer, and gay rights. Ultimately, however, the GOP's growing conservatism sparked a backlash among moderate-to-liberal Republicans in the Northeast and elsewhere. The end result of this realignment was a party system in which the ideological differences between the parties were much sharper and the regional bases of the two parties were reversed. By the end of the twentieth century the conservative South had become a

---

[19]Campbell, Converse, Miller, and Stokes, *The American Voter*, chapter 10.

[20]See Kevin Phillips, *The Emerging Republican Majority* (New Rochelle, NY: Arlington House, 1969).

Republican stronghold while the liberal Northeast had become the most strongly Democratic region of the nation.[21]

The ideological realignment of the party system meant that voters would receive much clearer cues from candidates and officeholders about the ideological positions of the parties. At the same time, rising levels of education among the American public meant that the voters themselves were better able to understand the ideological cues that they were receiving.

In his research on ideological thinking in the American public in the 1950s, Converse found that education was a powerful predictor of ideological sophistication—college graduates were much more likely than those with only a grade school or high school education to understand ideological concepts and to take consistent positions on issues. And in the half century since Converse conducted his research, there has been a dramatic change in educational attainment in the American public. Between the 1950s and the first decade of the twenty-first century, according to data from American National Election Studies surveys, college graduates increased from only 8 percent of the voting-age population to 26 percent, while those with only a grade school education fell from 34 percent of the voting-age population to only 3 percent.

Based on the growing clarity of party differences at the elite level and rising levels of education, one would expect the level of ideological sophistication of the public to have increased considerably over the past half century. In addition to these changes, however, one other trend has undoubtedly contributed to both increased awareness of party differences and growing ideological polarization among the public—the changing structure of the mass communications media. With the rise of cable television, talk radio, and the Internet, Americans now have easy access to a much greater variety of political information sources than in the past. And many of these sources provide information with a strongly partisan

---

[21]For an account of this transformation see Earl Black and Merle Black, *The Rise of Southern Republicans* (Cambridge: Harvard University Press, 2002) and Ronald Brownstein, *The Second Civil War: How Extreme Partisanship Has Paralyzed Washington and Polarized America* (New York: The Penguin Press, 2007). For a discussion of the new regional alignment of the party system, see Earl Black and Merle Black, *Divided America: The Ferocious Power Struggle in American Politics* (New York: Simon & Schuster, 2007).

and ideological coloration. While the proportion of Americans regularly reading a daily newspaper or tuning in to a network evening news broadcast has fallen considerably over the past several decades, the proportion listening to talk radio, reading liberal or conservative blogs on the Internet, or watching ideologically tinged cable television programs has increased dramatically.[22]

The issues that divide the parties have also changed over the past half century. Along with the traditional issues involving the role of government in regulating economic activity and providing a social safety net for those left behind by the normal operation of a capitalist economy, differences over the role of the United States in the world and especially the use of American military power have increased since the end of the Cold War. At the same time, a new set of issues has emerged in American politics in recent decades. These are issues that were rarely if ever discussed by candidates and party leaders during the 1950s and 1960s, issues such as abortion and gay marriage, which divide Americans along religious and cultural lines rather than along economic or class lines.

For many Americans today, cultural issues have a stronger influence on party identification and voting decisions than economic or foreign policy issues. Over time, the party divide on these issues has become sharper as the positions of party leaders have become more consistent across different issue domains. Today, almost all prominent Democratic leaders are both cultural economic liberals while almost all prominent Republican leaders are both cultural and economic conservatives.

This is true even within the Tea Party movement. While the initial focus of the movement during 2009 and 2010 was on issues of government spending and regulation, most of the politicians closely associated with the movement today, such as Minnesota Congresswoman Michele Bachmann, South Carolina Senator Jim DeMint, and Texas Governor Rick Perry, are strong cultural conservatives as well as strong economic

---

[22]For a discussion of these trends and their political consequences, see Markus Prior, *Post-Broadcast Democracy: How Media Choice Increases Inequality in Political Involvement and Polarizes Elections* (New York: Cambridge University Press, 2007). See also Diane C. Mutz, "How the Mass Media Divide Us," in *Red and Blue Nation? Characteristics and Causes of America's Polarized Politics*, ed. Petro S. Nivola and David W. Brady (Washington, DC: Brookings Institution Press, 2006), 223–48.

conservatives. Moreover, surveys indicate that supporters of the movement are overwhelmingly conservative on cultural as well as economic issues.[23]

Perhaps the most important long-term trend contributing to the rise of polarization in twenty-first-century America is the growing racial and ethnic diversity of the American population. Just between 1992 and 2008, the nonwhite share of the U.S. electorate doubled, from 13 to 26 percent. Moreover, according to the most recent census data, nonwhites now make up close to half of the U.S. population under the age of 5 compared to less than 10 percent of the population over the age of 70. Latinos make up about a quarter of the under-age-5 population today compared with less than 5 percent of the over-age-70 population. So regardless of future trends in immigration, the nonwhite, especially the Latino, share of the population and the electorate is certain to continue growing over the next few decades. In fact, Census Bureau projections indicate that by 2050, nonwhites, including Latinos, will constitute a majority of the U.S. population as they already do in the two most populous states in the nation—California and Texas.

The growing racial and ethnic diversity of the electorate has had major consequences for American politics. Without this shift, Barack Obama would never have become the nation's first African-American president. In 2008, Obama lost the white vote by a margin of more than eleven million votes but won the nonwhite vote by a margin of more than twenty million votes. More fundamentally, the movement of nonwhite voters into the Democratic Party and the corresponding movement of conservative white voters out of the Democratic Party and into the Republican Party have both transformed party coalitions and contributed to ideological polarization. The Democratic electoral coalition today is dominated by nonwhites and white liberals who strongly support activist government; the Republican electoral coalition is dominated by white conservatives who strongly oppose activist government, especially activist government that is seen as primarily benefiting nonwhites. We will examine the growing racial and ethnic diversity of the American electorate and its consequences for polarization in much greater depth in the next chapter.

---

[23]Williamson, Skocpol, and Coggin, "The Tea Party and the Remaking of Republican Conservatism," *Perspectives on Politics* 9 (March 2011), 25–44.

CHAPTER 2

The Racial Divide

He doesn't look like all those other presidents on the dollar bills.
—Barack Obama, referring to himself in
a campaign speech, July 30, 2008

Raising the issue of race in American politics is fraught with peril even if you're the first African-American presidential candidate of a major political party, or perhaps, especially if you're the first African-American presidential candidate of a major political party. Thus, Barack Obama's casual suggestion at a campaign rally in Missouri that some Republican strategists would try to use his race to frighten white voters was immediately met with a barrage of criticism from conservative pundits as well as from his Republican opponent, John McCain. Obama's decision to mention the issue of race, even in a humorous way, was denounced by his critics as an attempt to "play the race card" in order to discredit his opponents.[1] Whether that was his intent or not, the comment stood out because it was so unusual. Barack Obama rarely mentioned his race during the campaign. Moreover, he seldom addressed racial issues except when

---

[1] For an excellent account of the controversy, see Brendan Nyhan's blog post from August 4, 2008, "Obama's Dollar Bill Comment Triply Distorted," at http://www.brendan-nyhan.com/blog/2008/08/obamas-comment.html.

compelled to do so, as he was after the publication of racially charged statements by his former pastor, Jeremiah Wright.[2]

As a candidate for president, Barack Obama consistently tried to downplay the significance of racial issues and of his own mixed racial background during his battle for the Democratic nomination with Hillary Clinton and during the general election campaign. His goal was to persuade Americans to see him not as a black presidential candidate but as a presidential candidate who happened to be black. Yet there is little doubt that Obama's race, and the fact that his father was African and his mother was white, had a powerful impact on the 2008 presidential election and has had a powerful impact on his presidency. His remarkable rise to the White House was both helped and hindered by his racial identity and by the changing role of race in American politics. More fundamentally, there is little doubt that race has also been a major factor in the rise of polarization in American politics.

A century and a half after the end of slavery and almost fifty years after the end of legal segregation, race continues to divide Americans. While there has been much progress in race relations since the 1960s, as the election of the first African-American president clearly demonstrates, many problems remain. Housing patterns remain heavily segregated along racial lines in much of the country; large proportions of African-American and Latino students continue to attend segregated, and in many cases, inferior schools; African-Americans and Latinos make up a disproportionate share of the U.S. prison population; and the incomes of African-American and Latino families continue to lag far behind those of white

---

[2]Obama's response to the Jeremiah Wright controversy was a lengthy speech on the state of race relations in the United States in Philadelphia. The speech was generally praised by political commentators as a thoughtful attempt to address this very sensitive subject and the controversy, which had threatened to derail his candidacy, quickly died down. Despite the widespread praise for the Philadelphia speech, however, Obama seldom returned to the subject of race relations during the rest of the nomination campaign or the general election campaign. For a description of the Jeremiah Wright episode, see Jodi Cantor, "The Wright Controversy," which was published in The Caucus, the *New York Times* politics and government blog, on March 13, 2008: http://thecaucus.blogs.nytimes.com/2008/03/13/the-wright-controversy/. The Wright controversy and Obama's overall approach to the issue of race during the 2008 campaign are also discussed at length in John Heilemann and Mark Halperin, *Game Change: Obama and the Clintons, McCain and Palin, and the Race of a Lifetime* (New York: Harper, 2010).

families. Finally, African-Americans and Latinos are much less likely than whites to have health insurance coverage and, partly as a result, their life expectancy is considerably less than that of whites.[3]

Race continues to divide Americans politically as well. In fact, despite the unquestionable progress that the United States has made in the area of race relations over the past half century, the divide may be greater today than at any time in American history. In the decades since the passage of the federal Voting Rights Act in 1965, the Democratic Party has become increasingly dependent on the votes of African-Americans, Latinos, and other nonwhites. The increasing visibility and influence of nonwhites within the Democratic Party has contributed to the movement of the party's conservative whites into the Republican Party, which has welcomed the defectors with open arms. And while much of this white flight from the Democratic Party has been motivated by ideology, some of it undoubtedly has been motivated by racial fear and resentment. As a result of this movement, as well as the movement of African-Americans and liberal whites into the Democratic Party, the parties' electoral coalitions have become increasingly distinct in terms of both race and ideology.

Over the past half century, as conservative whites have fled the Democratic Party, the Democratic electoral coalition has become increasingly dominated by white liberals and nonwhites. According to data from

---

[3]For an excellent and comprehensive overview of the changing state of race relations in the United States, see Paula S. Rothenberg, ed., *Race, Class and Gender in the United States: An Integrated Study*, 8th edition (New York: Worth Publishing, 2010). On continued racial segregation in housing, see James H. Carr and Nandinee Kutty, eds., *Segregation: The Rising Costs for America* (New York: Routledge, 2008). On racial segregation in the public schools and its consequences, see Barry A. Gold, *Still Separate and Unequal: Segregation and the Future of Urban School Reform* (New York: Teachers College Press, 2007). For evidence on differences in rates of incarceration in the United Sates by race, see the report from Human Rights Watch, "Race and Incarceration in the United States" (February 27, 2002): http://www.hrw.org/legacy/backgrounder/usa/race/. See also, Glenn C. Loury with Pamela S. Karlan, Tommie Shelby, and Loic Wacquant, *Race, Incarceration and American Values* (Cambridge: Massachusetts Institute of Technology Press, 2008). For evidence on racial disparities in income, education, and home ownership, see CBS News, "Report: Race Gap in U.S. Persists" (February 11, 2009): http://www.cbsnews.com/stories/2006/11/14/national/main2179601 .shtml. Finally, for evidence on race, health insurance, and life expectancy, see James B. Kirby and Toshiko Kaneda, "Unhealthy and Uninsured: Exploring Racial Differences in Health and Health Insurance Coverage Using a Life Table Approach," *Demography* 47 (November 2010): 1035–51.

American National Election Study (ANES) surveys, between 1972, the first election in which the ideology question was included in the survey, and 2008, the percentage of Democratic voters belonging to these two groups rose from 44 to 71 percent. At the same time, the Republican electoral coalition was becoming increasingly dominated by one group—white conservatives. According to the ANES data, between 1972 and 2008, the percentage of white conservatives among Republican voters increased from 54 to 74 percent. If we could go back to the 1950s, the shift would undoubtedly be even more dramatic. This transformation of the parties' coalitions has had profound consequences for electoral competition in the United States, as the results of the 2008 presidential election clearly demonstrate. Barack Obama's election as the first African-American president was a direct result of the racial transformation of the American party system over the past half century.

THE RACIAL DIVIDE IN 2008

Barack Obama won the 2008 presidential election by a fairly decisive margin—outpolling John McCain by a little over 7 percentage points in the national popular vote, or more than 9.5 million votes. It was the largest percentage margin for a winning presidential candidate since Bill Clinton in 1996 and the largest raw vote margin since Ronald Reagan in 1984. But Obama's decisive victory was based entirely on his overwhelming margin among African-Americans and other nonwhite voters. According to the 2008 national exit poll, Obama won only 43 percent of the white vote compared with 55 percent for John McCain. That twelve-point deficit among white voters was considerably better than John Kerry's eighteen-point deficit among white voters in 2004, but it was about the same as Al Gore's deficit among white voters in 2000.

The fact that Barack Obama lost the white vote to John McCain in 2008 is hardly surprising. No Democratic presidential candidate has carried the white vote since Lyndon Johnson in 1964, although Jimmy Carter in 1976 and Bill Clinton in both 1992 and 1996 came much closer than Obama. But the margin by which Obama lost the white vote in 2008 was somewhat surprising given both the poor condition of the U.S. economy and the extraordinary unpopularity of the incumbent Republican president, George W. Bush, at the time of the election.

An economy in the depths of the worst recession since the Great Depression and a Republican president with an approval rating hovering around 30 percent might have led one to expect the Democratic presidential candidate to do better than a double-digit loss among white voters. And while Obama did improve on John Kerry's performance among white voters in most of the country, that was not true everywhere. In several states in the Deep South and Appalachia, the Democratic share of the white vote actually declined between 2004 and 2008. In Alabama, Mississippi, and Louisiana, exit polls found that Obama did even worse than Kerry, winning only a little over 10 percent of the white vote. And in Arkansas, Tennessee, and Oklahoma, Obama lost the white vote by a larger margin than any Democratic presidential candidate since Michael Dukakis in 1988.

It is difficult to explain why Barack Obama would have done even worse than John Kerry among white voters in the Deep South and Appalachia without taking into account the impact of lingering racial fear and resentment. Old-fashioned racist attitudes are rarely expressed in public in American society today, but there is evidence from recent public opinion surveys that racial resentment—a feeling that blacks receive special treatment and benefits that they don't deserve—is still fairly common in some segments of white society.[4] For example, in the 2008 ANES survey, 12 percent of white respondents expressed the belief that blacks in the United States had too much political influence—a belief that is hard to square with the fact that African-Americans continue to

---

[4]See for example, Alan I. Abramowitz, "The Race Factor: White Racial Attitudes and Opinions of Obama," *Sabato's Crystal Ball* (May 12, 2011): http://www.centerforpolitics.org/crystalball/articles/aia2011051201/. For a comprehensive but slightly outdated study of racial attitudes in the United States, see Howard Schuman, Charlotte Steeh, Lawrence Bobo, and Maria Krysan, *Racial Attitudes in America: Trends and Interpretations*, revised edition (Cambridge: Harvard University Press, 1997). A brief update of some of these data can be found at Maria Krysan and Nakesha Faison, "Racial Attitudes in America: A Brief Summary of the Updated Data," University of Illinois Institute of Government and Public Affairs: http://igpa.uillinois.edu/programs/racial-attitudes/brief.

be underrepresented in positions of political leadership in the federal government and in many state governments. This opinion was considerably more common among white Republicans (18 percent) and conservatives (20 percent) than among white Democrats (6 percent) and liberals (4 percent).

Not surprisingly, Barack Obama fared very poorly among white voters who felt that blacks in the United States had too much political influence—losing to John McCain by a margin of 88 percent to 12 percent. Among the small group of white Democrats who felt that blacks had too much influence, Obama received only 54 percent of the vote versus more than 90 percent among all other white Democrats. These results suggest that attitudes of racial resentment had an impact on Obama's performance among white voters in some parts of the country.

Obviously, Barack Obama's relatively weak showing among white voters wasn't enough to derail his candidacy. That was because his overwhelming margin among African-American and other nonwhite voters more than offset his deficit among white voters. According to the national exit poll data, Obama won 95 percent of the African-American vote, 67 percent of the Latino vote, and 62 percent of the Asian-American vote. Altogether, Obama won over 80 percent of the nonwhite vote in 2008. In raw numbers, we can estimate based on the exit poll results that while Obama lost to John McCain by about eleven million votes among whites, he defeated McCain by more than twenty-one million votes among nonwhites. That unprecedented margin among nonwhites—almost twice as large as that of any previous Democratic presidential candidate including Bill Clinton—was what allowed Barack Obama to win the national popular vote by a decisive margin and to win a landslide victory in the Electoral College. But the gap between Obama's support among whites and his support among nonwhites was larger than that of any Democratic presidential candidate in more than a quarter century. According to data from the ANES, the forty-four-point gap between Obama's share of the white vote and his share of the nonwhite vote was the largest for any Democratic candidate since Jimmy Carter in 1980. It was the largest for any winning Democratic candidate since World War II.

THE RACIAL TRANSFORMATION OF THE
AMERICAN PARTY SYSTEM

American society today is very different from the society that existed in the 1950s when Philip Converse and his coauthors were conducting their path-breaking research on public opinion and voting behavior in the United States. In that America, the large majority of families consisted of a married couple with children and divorce was relatively rare, husbands were considered the breadwinners in the family and wives were expected to stay home with the children at least until they completed their school-ing, abortion was illegal in most states, homosexuals were expected to stay in the closet, and blacks in most of the South could be arrested if they tried to eat in a white restaurant or ride in the front of a bus. Black people were also largely barred from voting in most of the southern states by a combination of legal and informal barriers including white-only prima-ries, poll taxes, literacy tests, and, when necessary, violence.[5]

Where they could vote, a large percentage of African-Americans con-tinued to support the party of Abraham Lincoln in the years following World War II. While Franklin Roosevelt had brought African-Americans into his New Deal coalition in the 1930s and 1940s by providing jobs and other benefits to African-Americans who were among those hardest hit by the Great Depression, many black people continued to view the Democratic Party, especially in the South, as the party of white supremacy and Jim Crow. It is easy to forget today that as recently as 1960, accord-ing to ANES, Republican presidential candidate Richard Nixon received about a third of the African-American vote against his Democratic oppo-nent, John F. Kennedy.

But any lingering attachment of African-Americans to the Republican Party came to an end in the 1960s. The full-throated commitment of Democratic President Lyndon Johnson to the cause of civil rights; the pas-sage of the most significant civil rights laws since the end of Reconstruction, including the 1965 Voting Rights Act, by the Democratic Congress; and

---

[5]On the history of the struggle for the black franchise, see Alexander Keyssar, *The Right to Vote: The Contested History of Democracy in the United States* (New York: Basic Books, 2000), chapter 8.

the 1964 presidential election, in which Republican presidential nominee Barry Goldwater for the first time put his party clearly on record in opposition to the cause of civil rights, moved African-American voters solidly into the Democratic camp.

Although blacks made up only 8 percent of the national electorate in 1964, they cast their ballots nearly unanimously for Lyndon Johnson. In fact, in the 1964 ANES survey, not a single black respondent admitted voting for Barry Goldwater. In every presidential election since 1964, blacks have voted overwhelmingly, usually by margins close to 90–10, for the Democratic nominee. Even George McGovern in 1972 received close to 90 percent of the black vote in his landslide loss to Richard Nixon. Thus, Barack Obama's 95 percent share of the African-American vote in 2008 was only slightly higher than the recent average.[6]

Just before signing the landmark 1964 Civil Rights Act, which ended Jim Crow laws by guaranteeing African-Americans access to public accommodations, Lyndon Johnson is reported to have commented to his aide Bill Moyers that, "I think we have just delivered the South to the Republican Party for a long time to come." Johnson's statement, if he actually made it, turned out to be less than totally prescient. In fact, Johnson himself carried most of the South in the 1964 presidential election, losing only four states in the Deep South—Mississippi, Alabama, Louisiana, and Georgia. Other Democratic presidential candidates since Johnson, including Jimmy Carter in 1976 and Bill Clinton in both 1992 and 1996, have also enjoyed some success in the South and after 1965 Democrats continued to hold a majority of House and Senate seats from the South for another thirty years. In 2008, Barack Obama carried three southern states—Florida, Virginia, and North Carolina.

But while the South did not completely abandon the Democratic Party after 1964, the Republican Party clearly has become the dominant party in the region as a result of the shifting party loyalties of white voters. In the 1950s, according to ANES data, 75 percent of white voters in the

---

[6]On the recent history of African-American support for the Democratic Party, see Katherine Tate, *From Protest to Politics: The New Black Voters in American Elections*, enlarged edition (New York: Russell Sage Foundation, 1994).

South identified with the Democratic Party while only 19 percent identified with the Republican Party. By the first decade of the twenty-first
century, however, only 32 percent of white voters identified with the
Democratic Party while 61 percent identified with the GOP. The growing
Republican identification of southern white voters and their growing support for Republican candidates for president, Congress, governor, state
legislature, and local offices has transformed southern politics. It has also
had a profound impact on national politics, contributing to the growing
conservatism of the Republican Party.[7]

THE RISE OF THE NONWHITE ELECTORATE

American society in the 1950s was very different from American society in
the twenty-first century in another respect—it was overwhelmingly white.
And since a large proportion of African-Americans who lived in the South
were barred from voting, the American electorate of the 1950s was even
more overwhelmingly white. According to the 1950 census, nonwhites
of all types made up barely 10 percent of the U.S. population. Almost
all nonwhites in 1950 were African-American. Less than 1 percent of the
population consisted of Asian-Americans or Native-Americans. Latinos
were not even counted as a separate category in the census.

As a result of immigration, both legal and illegal, and higher birth
rates among racial minorities, the nonwhite share of the U.S. population
has increased substantially in the past half century, with the most dramatic growth occurring since 1980. According to the 2010 census, nonwhites made up 36 percent of the overall population. Of that 36 percent,
13 percent was made up of African-Americans; 16 percent was made up
of Latinos, who are by far the fastest growing segment of the U.S. population; and 5 percent was made up of Asian-Americans.

The growth of the nonwhite electorate has lagged considerably
behind the growth of the nonwhite population, however, as a result of

---

[7]For a brilliant analysis of the growth of the Republican Party in the South and its impact on national
politics, see Earl Black and Merle Black, *The Rise of Southern Republicans* (Cambridge: Harvard
University Press, 2002).

a high proportion of noncitizens and a high proportion of individuals under the age of 18 as well as lower rates of registration and turnout. Nevertheless, the data from ANES surveys displayed in Figure 2.1 show that the nonwhite share of the U.S. electorate has increased considerably over the past several decades. In the 1950s, nonwhites made up only 5 percent of all voters. By the first decade of the twenty-first century, non-whites made up almost 25 percent of all voters. African-Americans went from less than 5 percent of voters in the 1950s to more than 12 percent in the 2000s, while Latinos and other nonwhites went from less than 1 percent of voters in the 1950s to more than 11 percent in the 2000s.

Data from national exit polls show a trend similar to the ANES data. Just between 1992 and 2008, the nonwhite share of the U.S. electorate doubled, going from 13 to 26 percent. Barack Obama's candidacy undoubtedly contributed to an unusually strong turnout among black

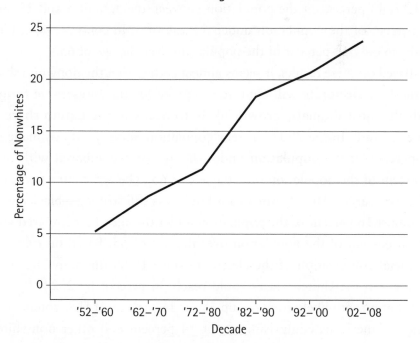

FIGURE 2.1

Trend in Nonwhite Percentage of the U.S. Electorate

Source: American National Election Studies, 1952–2008

voters in 2008—African-Americans made up a record 13 percent of the electorate in 2008, up from 11 percent in 2004. But the overall increase in the nonwhite share of the electorate between 2004 and 2008 was in line with the trend since 1992. And an examination of the 2008 exit poll data as well as recent census data make it clear that there is no reason to expect the growth of nonwhite electorate to end any time soon.

According to the 2008 national exit poll, the nonwhite share of the electorate was considerably larger among younger age groups than among older age groups. The younger the age group, the larger the nonwhite share of voters. Thus, nonwhites made up 40 percent of voters under the age of 25 versus only 14 percent of voters over the age of 75. And the results of the 2007 Current Population Survey show that the nonwhite share of the age groups that will be entering the electorate over the next two decades is considerably larger than the nonwhite share of the oldest age groups in the electorate. As with the exit poll data, the younger the age group, the larger the nonwhite share of the population. Thus, nonwhites made up 40 percent of the population between the ages of 14 and 17, 43 percent of the population between the ages of 5 and 13, and 46 percent of the population under the age of 5. In contrast, nonwhites made up only 19 percent of the population over the age of 65.

Based on these results, it seems almost certain that the nonwhite share of the U.S. electorate will continue to grow for the foreseeable future, with the most dramatic growth likely to occur in the Latino share of the electorate. In the 2007 Current Population Survey, Latinos made up 24 percent of the population under the age of 5 compared with only 7 percent of the population over the age of 65. The age contrast was not quite as great for African-Americans but it was still striking—blacks made up almost 16 percent of the population under the age of 5 compared with only 8 percent of the population over the age of 65. Based on trends in the racial composition of the electorate since 1992, the nonwhite share of voters in the United States could reach 36 percent by 2024. By that time, Latinos are likely to make up about 16 percent of U.S. voters, with African-Americans comprising about 14 percent and other nonwhites, including Asian-Americans, comprising about 6 percent.

RACE AND THE RISE OF POLARIZATION

The growing racial diversity of the U.S. population has had profound consequences for American politics and American elections. For one thing, increased racial diversity made it possible for someone like Barack Obama to be elected to the presidency. If the racial composition of the American electorate in 2008 had been the same as the racial composition of the American electorate as recently as 1992, based on his share of the vote among various racial groups, Obama would have lost decisively to John McCain. Beyond the impact on the 2008 presidential election, growing racial diversity has also contributed to the rise of polarization in American politics. That is because the growing nonwhite share of the U.S. electorate has led to a growing racial divide between the Democratic and Republican electoral coalitions and this growing racial divide has been a major factor contributing to the growing ideological divide between the Democratic and Republican electoral coalitions.

Figure 2.2 displays the trends in the nonwhite percentages of Democratic and Republican voters over the past six decades based on data from the ANES. Over this time period, the nonwhite share of Democratic voters has increased dramatically, going from only 7 percent in the 1950s to 36 percent in the 2000s. Meanwhile, the nonwhite share of Republican voters has increased only slightly, going from 3 percent in the 1950s to 10 percent in the 2000s. As a result, the racial divide between supporters of the two parties has widened, from a very narrow gap in the 1950s to a yawning chasm in the twenty-first century.

The data from the 2008 national exit poll confirm these trends. Nonwhites made up 39 percent of Obama voters versus only 10 percent of McCain voters. Most strikingly, African-Americans made up 23 percent of Obama voters compared with only 1 percent of McCain voters. Despite the efforts of Republican leaders to expand their party's appeal beyond its white base and to place members of minority groups in highly visible leadership positions, including the chairmanship of the Republican National Committee, the two major parties in the United States today present a stark contrast in terms of their racial profiles. As anyone who has

FIGURE 2.2

Trends in Nonwhite Percentages of Democratic and Republican Voters

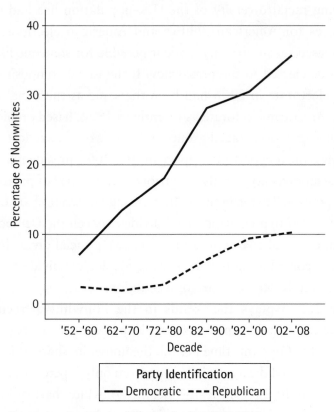

Source: American National Election Studies, 1952–2008

attended or watched party conventions or campaign rallies in recent years knows, supporters of the two parties look very different. In twenty-first-century America, we have a two-party system that consists of a racially diverse Democratic Party and an overwhelmingly white Republican Party.

Not only is the racial divide between supporters of the two major parties now enormous, it is likely to grow even larger over the next several election cycles. That is because the racial divide between the parties' electoral coalitions is much larger among younger voters than it is among older voters. This can be seen in Table 2.1, which compares the racial composition of Obama and McCain voters per the 2008 national exit poll by age. While nonwhites were much more prevalent among Obama voters than among McCain voters in every age group, the gap

TABLE 2.1

Nonwhite Percentage of Obama and McCain Voters
by Age in 2008

AGE GROUP	OBAMA VOTERS (%)	McCAIN VOTERS (%)
18–29	49	14
30–44	45	12
45–64	33	9
65+	26	7

Source: 2008 National Exit Poll

between the candidates' supporters was far greater in the youngest age group than it was in the oldest age group. Among voters over the age of 65, nonwhites made up 26 percent of Obama voters compared with 7 percent of McCain voters. But among voters under the age of 30, nonwhites made up 49 percent of Obama voters compared with 14 percent of McCain voters.

Latinos are now the fastest growing segment of the U.S. electorate. According to data from the ANES, the Latino share of the U.S. electorate grew from less than 1 percent in 1972 to 7 percent in 2008. In the southwestern states, including Texas and California, Latinos already comprise by far the largest minority voting bloc. According to state exit polls, Barack Obama would not have carried Nevada or New Mexico without the overwhelming support of Latino voters, and his margin in Colorado would have been very narrow. And over the next twenty to thirty years, the Latino share of the U.S. electorate is expected to continue growing. By 2016, if not sooner, Latinos will probably comprise a larger voting bloc than African-Americans.

The continued growth of the Latino electorate and the close balance of support between the Democratic and Republican parties in the nation mean that the outcomes of future national elections in the United States will depend heavily on Latino votes. In the past, both major parties have actively courted Latino voters. Traditionally, Latinos, while leaning Democratic, have divided their votes between the two major parties much more evenly than African-Americans, with a third or more sometimes supporting Republican candidates. According to data from the national exit poll, as recently as 2004, George W. Bush won well over 40 percent of the Latino vote.

The political diversity of the Latino electorate reflects, in part, the economic and cultural diversity of the Latino population in the United States.[8] For example, Cuban-Americans in Florida have traditionally supported Republican candidates at the state and national levels based on a strong legacy of anticommunist sentiment while Mexican-Americans in California have generally tilted strongly Democratic. Similarly, affluent Latinos have been more likely to vote Republican than lower income Latinos. However, the steady rightward drift of the Republican Party and especially the party's increasingly hard-line position on the issue of immigration are now threatening to undermine future Latino support for the GOP. According to data from the 2008 ANES, more than two-thirds of Latino voters support comprehensive immigration reform, including a path to citizenship—a position rejected by almost all prominent Republican leaders and by nearly two-thirds of white Republican voters. Moreover, among the large majority of Latino voters who consider immigration reform a very or extremely important issue, over 80 percent favor comprehensive reform including a path to citizenship.

The growing size of the nonwhite electorate and the steady rightward drift of the Republican Party almost guarantee that the nonwhite share of Democratic electoral base will continue to grow over the next several election cycles. And this trend should, in turn, continue to drive conservative and racially resentful whites into the Republican camp, thereby pushing the GOP even further to the right. In fact, we don't have to wait to see evidence of this trend—we have already seen this dynamic at work in the rise of the Tea Party movement following the 2008 election.

Evidence from a new data set, the American National Election Study Evaluations of Government and Society Survey, shows very clearly that both conservatism and racial resentment contributed to the emergence of

---

[8]Marisa A. Abrajano and R. Michael Alvarez, *New Faces, New Voices: The Hispanic Electorate in America* (Princeton: Princeton University Press, 2010).

the Tea Party movement during 2009 and 2010. According to data from the October 2010 wave of the Evaluations of Government and Society Survey (EGSS) Tea Party supporters made up close to a quarter of the overall electorate and close to half of Republican identifiers. Almost all Tea Party supporters were Republicans but Tea Party supporters scored considerably higher than other Republicans on measures of both conservatism and racial resentment. These data suggest that, in addition to strong opposition to the economic policies of the new Democratic president and Congress, the presence of an African-American in the White House and the growing visibility and influence of nonwhites in the Democratic Party motivated many Republicans to become involved in the Tea Party movement.[9]

THE RACIAL DIVIDE AND IDEOLOGICAL POLARIZATION

In a society in which race continues to be strongly related to many vital areas of life, including housing, education, health care and economic opportunity, the existence of a large racial divide between the two major political parties is itself of major importance. But the importance of the racial divide is compounded by the fact that it corresponds to a deep divide on many important political issues, especially those involving the role of government in American society.

Perhaps the most enduring issues dividing Democrats from Republicans are those involving the role of government in American society. These issues include the scope of government regulation of private economic activity, the level of government spending and taxation, and the generosity of social welfare programs that benefit the sick, the elderly, and those in need. On these issues, as the data in Table 2.2 from the 2008 ANES show, African-Americans and Latinos consistently support activist government to a much greater degree than white-Americans.

---

[9]Alan I. Abramowitz, "Grand Old Tea Party: Partisan Polarization and the Rise of the Tea Party Movement." Paper prepared for delivery at the Annual Meeting of the American Political Science Association, Seattle, WA, September 1–4, 2011. See also Vanessa Williamson, Theda Skocpol, and John Coggin, "The Tea Party and the Remaking of Republican Conservatism," *Perspectives on Politics* 9 (March 2011): 25–44.

TABLE 2.2
Voter Support for Activist Government by Race in 2008

ISSUE	WHITES (%)	BLACKS (%)	HISPANICS (%)
SERVICES AND SPENDING	42	67	66
JOBS AND LIVING STANDARDS	22	57	48
UNIVERSAL HEALTH CARE	42	65	71
GOVERNMENT DO MORE OR LESS	48	86	79
GUN CONTROL	41	64	67

Source: 2008 American National Election Study

One of the most striking differences between whites and nonwhites in responses to these issues was on the general question of whether there were more things government should be doing or whether government was already doing too many things best left to the private sector. On this question, despite the ongoing financial crisis and the dire condition of the U.S. economy, white voters in 2008 were fairly evenly divided with slightly more respondents taking the view that government was doing too many things best left to the private sector. In contrast, overwhelming majorities of both African-American and Latino voters took the position that government needed to be doing more to address societal ills.

There are good reasons to expect the racial divide in public opinion to remain sizeable for the foreseeable future. Survey data show that younger nonwhites today are at least as liberal in political outlook as their elders. In fact, the data in Table 2.3, from the 2008 ANES survey, show that on some cultural issues, younger nonwhites, like younger whites, are considerably more liberal than their elders. Thus, nonwhite voters under the age of 30 were much more likely to support same-sex marriage than those over the age of 40. This was true of both younger Latinos and younger African-Americans. And on issues involving government regulation, spending, and services, younger nonwhites were every bit as liberal as their elders.

TABLE 2.3

Liberalism of Nonwhite Voters in 2008 by Age

ISSUE	18–29 (%)	30–39 (%)	40 AND OLDER (%)
SERVICES AND SPENDING	75	66	66
JOBS AND LIVING STANDARDS	53	46	54
UNIVERSAL HEALTH CARE	80	64	63
GOVERNMENT DO MORE OR LESS	83	80	81
GUN CONTROL	63	55	68
GAY MARRIAGE	63	46	24
ABORTION	46	46	41

Source: 2008 American National Election Study

CHAPTER SUMMARY

The growing dependence of the Democratic Party on nonwhite votes over the past half century, and especially since the 1980s, has served to reinforce the commitment of Democratic candidates and officeholders to activist government and especially to government programs that benefit minority communities. And this trend has also had a major impact on the Republican Party. The perception of a Democratic Party committed to liberal social programs and increasingly dependent on nonwhite votes has helped to drive more and more conservative and racially resentful white voters into the Republican fold. The end result of both of these trends, as we will see in Chapter 3, is growing ideological polarization—an increasingly liberal Democratic electorate and an increasingly conservative Republican electorate.

CHAPTER 3

The Ideological Divide

I think [the Democrats] have always helped the farmers.... We have always had good times under their Administration. They are more for the working class of people. I think the Republicans favor the richer folks.

—Ohio farm woman interviewed for the 1956
American National Election Study[1]

Amerian politics hasn't always revolved around ideology. In the American electorate of the 1950s, the most important political cleavages were based on class, region, and religion. After capturing the presidency for the Democratic Party in 1932, in the midst of the worst economic crisis in American history, Franklin Roosevelt forged a coalition that dominated American politics for more than three decades. Roosevelt's New Deal policies resulted in a dramatic expansion in the role of the federal government in many areas of American life.[2] Yet from the standpoint of the average voter, the appeal of the Democratic Party during those years was based less on an ideology of governmental activism than on the concrete benefits that the New Deal provided to those who had been hard hit by the Great Depression—benefits such as public works projects,

---

[1]Quoted in Angus Campbell, Philip E. Converse, Warren E. Miller, and Donald E. Stokes, *The American Voter* (New York: John Wiley & Sons, 1960), p. 236.

[2]For an excellent overview of the New Deal and its impact on the American public, see David M. Kennedy, *Freedom from Fear: The American People in Depression and War, 1929–1945* (New York: Oxford University Press, 1999).

rural electrification, and agricultural price supports—and the association of Republicans with hard times and the Democrats with prosperity.

More than two decades after Roosevelt's first election, in surveys conducted by the American National Election Studies (ANES) between 1952 and 1960, the twin themes of group benefits and the goodness or badness of the times dominated Americans' responses to a series of open-ended questions asking what they liked or disliked about the two major parties. In contrast, references to the parties' ideological positions or policies were relatively rare.[3]

Despite Republican Dwight Eisenhower's decisive victories in the 1952 and 1956 presidential elections, Roosevelt's New Deal coalition remained largely intact. Democrats enjoyed a large advantage in party identification in the national electorate during those years. According to the ANES surveys, Democrats and independents leaning toward the Democratic Party made up 54 percent of the electorate during the 1950s while Republicans and independents leaning toward the Republican Party made up only 39 percent.

The Democratic advantage was much larger among voters belonging to the three groups that formed the core of Roosevelt's electoral coalition: southern whites, northern white Catholics, and northern white blue-collar voters. According to the ANES data, during the 1950s, Democrats and Democratic-leaning independents outnumbered Republicans and Republican-leaning independents by 75 to 19 percent among southern whites, by 68 to 24 percent among northern white Catholics, and by 59 to 33 percent among northern white blue-collar voters.

IDEOLOGICAL REALIGNMENT AND THE DEMISE OF THE NEW DEAL PARTY SYSTEM

The first cracks in FDR's coalition began to emerge not long after his death in 1945. Not surprisingly, the issue that produced those cracks was race. In 1948, South Carolina governor J. Strom Thurmond led a walkout of

---

[3]Philip E. Converse, "The Nature of Belief Systems in Mass Publics," in *Ideology and Discontent*, ed. David Apter (New York: The Free Press of Glencoe, 1964). See also Campbell, Converse, Miller, and Stokes, *The American Voter*, chapter 9.

southern delegates from the Democratic National Convention over the adoption of a fairly mild civil rights plank introduced by Minneapolis mayor and liberal firebrand Hubert Humphrey. Rather than endorse Roosevelt's successor, Harry Truman, Thurmond and his followers formed the States Rights or Dixiecrat Party, with Thurmond as its standard-bearer, taking thirty-nine electoral votes in the Deep South from the Democrats.[4]

It was probably inevitable that a coalition including groups with as widely diverging policy preferences as southern segregationists and progressive trade unionists would eventually break apart. Truman won the 1948 presidential election despite the defection of the Dixiecrats but over the next several decades the cracks in the New Deal coalition would continue to expand as Republican politicians from Richard Nixon to Ronald Reagan sought to win over traditional Democrats dissatisfied with their party's liberal national leadership and policies.[5] Figure 3.1 displays the trends in party identification between the 1950s and the first decade of the twenty-first century of voters belonging to any of the three groups that had formed the core of Roosevelt's New Deal coalition—southern whites, northern white Catholics, and northern white blue-collar workers. Among voters belonging to these three groups, the data show a steady and dramatic decline in Democratic identification that began during the 1950s and has continued into the 2000s.

By the first decade of the twenty-first century, Democratic identification among northern white Catholics and northern blue-collar workers had fallen below 50 percent and southern whites had become one of the most Republican voting blocs in the electorate. In the 2008 presidential election, according to exit poll data, Barack Obama won only 30 percent of the vote among southern whites. In several states in the Deep South, including Alabama, Mississippi, and Louisiana, Obama won barely a tenth of the white vote.

---

[4]See Kari A. Frederickson, *The Dixiecrat Revolt and the End of the Solid South* (Chapel Hill: University of North Carolina Press, 2001). See also Nadine Cohodas, *Strom Thurmond and the Politics of Southern Change* (New York: Simon & Schuster, 1999) and Earl Black and Merle Black, *The Rise of Southern Republicans* (Cambridge: Harvard University Press, 2002).

[5]Earl Black and Merle Black, *Divided America: The Ferocious Power Struggle in American Politics* (New York: Simon & Schuster, 2007), chapter 1.

FIGURE 3.1

Trend in Party Identification of Key New Deal Coalition Groups

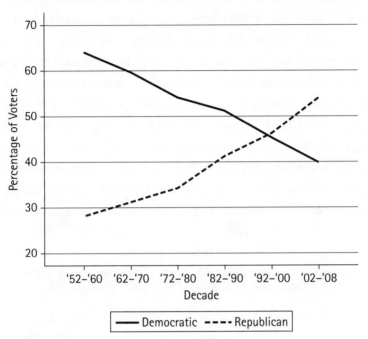

Source: American National Election Studies, 1952–2008

The decline of the New Deal coalition was part of a broader transformation of the American party system since the 1950s. Over several decades, a party system in which attachments to political parties were based primarily on membership in concrete social groups has been replaced by a party system in which attachments to political parties are based primarily on policy preferences and ideology. While supporters of the two major parties continue to differ in terms of their social characteristics, those differences are largely by-products of differences between the ideologies and policy preferences of members of various social groups. Group membership itself is no longer the prime determinant of party identification in the United States.[6]

---

[6]Alan I. Abramowitz and Kyle L. Saunders, "Exploring the Bases of Partisanship in the American Electorate: Social Identity vs. Ideology," *Political Research Quarterly* 59 (2006): 175–87.

The dramatic shifts in the party loyalties of social groups such as southern whites, northern white Catholics, and northern white blue-collar voters since the 1950s have been driven primarily by ideology. This is evident in Figure 3.2, which displays the trends in Democratic identification among liberals, moderates, and conservatives belonging to these three traditionally Democratic groups over the past four decades. Unfortunately, it is not possible to trace these shifts back earlier than the 1970s because the ANES surveys did not include an ideological identification question before 1972. We therefore cannot capture the rather substantial shifts in party identification that occurred between the 1950s and 1970s. Nevertheless, the results displayed in Figure 3.2 are very revealing. The decline in Democratic identification

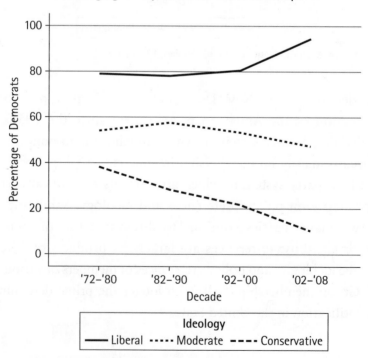

FIGURE 3.2

Trends in Democratic Identification by Ideology among Voters
Belonging to Key New Deal Coalition Groups

Source: American National Election Studies, 1952–2008

between the 1970s and the 2000s was concentrated disproportionately among conservatives. Among this group, Democratic identification fell from 40 percent in the 1970s to just over 10 percent in the 2000s. In contrast, there was only a modest decline in Democratic identification among moderates and an increase in Democratic identification among liberals.

Ideological realignment has not been limited to traditionally Democratic voter groups. As the Republican Party has gained ground among conservative voters in the South and elsewhere, voters with more liberal policy preferences have been moving away from the GOP. During the 1950s, northern white college graduates were one of the most staunchly Republican voter groups with Republican identifiers and Republican-leaning independents outnumbering Democratic identifiers and Democratic-leaning independents by a better than two-to-one margin, according to data from ANES surveys. By the first decade of the twenty-first century, however, the two parties enjoyed almost equal support among northern white college graduates. According to the ANES data, Republicans and independents leaning toward the Republican Party made up 49 percent of this group while Democrats and Democratic-leaning independents made up 48 percent.

As with the traditionally Democratic voter groups, the dramatic shift in the party loyalties of northern white college graduates was the result of an ideological realignment of party identification within this group. Figure 3.3 displays the trends in Democratic identification among liberal, moderate, and conservative northern white college graduates since the 1970s. Again, it is unfortunate that we cannot trace this shift back further in time since we are missing the fairly dramatic change that took place between the 1950s and 1970s. However, once again, the pattern is clear and consistent with the ideological realignment hypothesis. The increase in Democratic identification among northern white college graduates over these four decades was concentrated among liberals and moderates. Among conservatives, Democratic identification actually declined slightly during this time period.

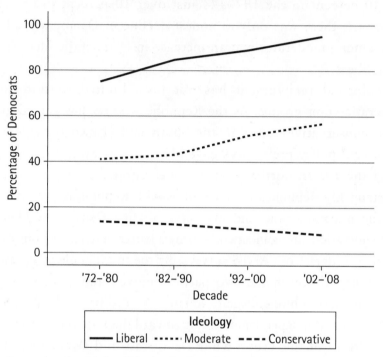

FIGURE 3.3

Trends in Democratic Identification by Ideology among
Northern White College Graduates

Ideology
—— Liberal ····· Moderate - - - Conservative

Source: American National Election Studies, 1952–2008

THE RISE OF IDEOLOGICAL POLARIZATION

The result of ideological realignment within the U.S. electorate over the
past half century has been a steady increase in the ideological distance
between supporters of the two major parties. As relatively conservative voters have shifted toward the Republican Party and relatively liberal voters
have shifted toward the Democratic Party, the average ideological position
of Democratic voters has moved to the left while the average ideological
position of Republican voters has moved to the right. This shift can be
seen very clearly in Figure 3.4 (see Chapter 3 color insert), which displays
the trend in the average location of Democratic and Republican voters on
the ANES seven-point liberal-conservative scale between the 1970s and

FIGURE 3.4

Average Positions of Democratic and Republican Voters on Liberal-Conservative Scale by Decade

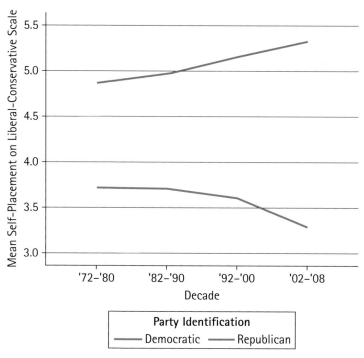

Source: American National Election Studies, 1952–2008

FIGURE 3.5
Illustration of Sorting without Polarization

a.

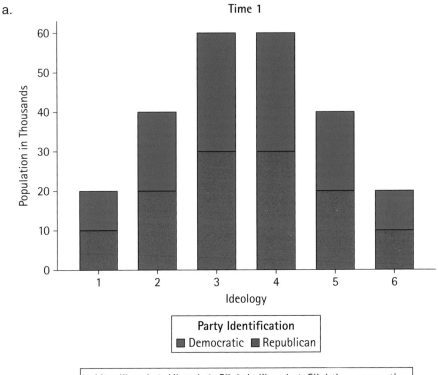

Time 1

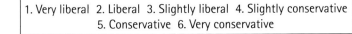

Party Identification
■ Democratic ■ Republican

1. Very liberal 2. Liberal 3. Slightly liberal 4. Slightly conservative
5. Conservative 6. Very conservative

b.

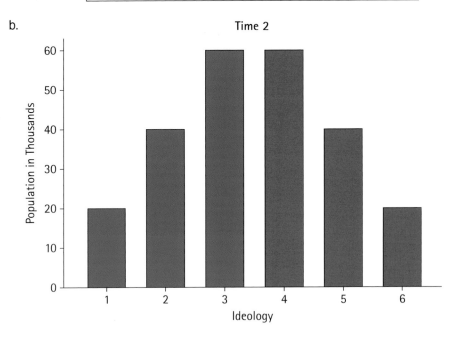

Time 2

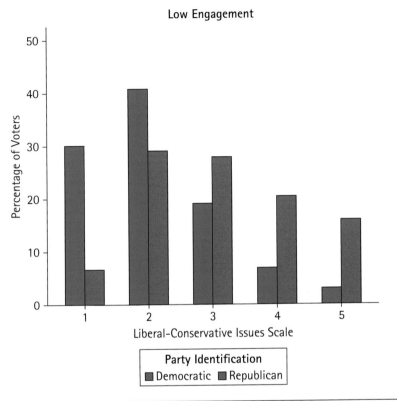

FIGURE 3.8
Party Sorting and Ideological Polarization by Political Engagement in 2010

a.

Low Engagement

Percentage of Voters

Liberal-Conservative Issues Scale

Party Identification
Democratic Republican

1. Very liberal 2. Liberal 3. Moderate 4. Conservative 5. Very conservative

FIGURE 3.8 (*Continued*)

b.

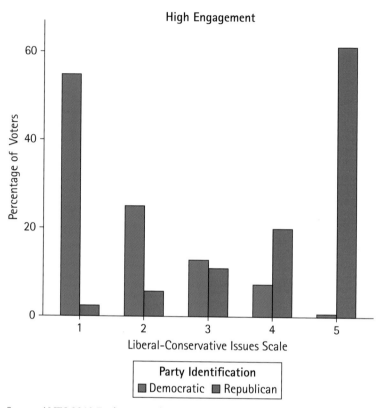

High Engagement

Source: ANES 2010 Evaluations of Government and Society Survey

the first decade of the twenty-first century. The scale has a maximum range of six units with position 1 labeled "extremely liberal" and position 7 labeled "extremely conservative."

Between 1972, the first election in this series, and 2008, the last election in this series, the gap between the average Democratic voter and the average Republican voter more than doubled, going from 1.0 unit to 2.2 units. The average Democratic voter moved from a mean location of 3.7 in 1972 to a mean location of 3.2 in the 2008 while the average Republican voter moved even further, from a mean location of 4.7 in 1972 to a mean location of 5.4 in 2008.

To put these shifts in more concrete terms, among Republican voters between 1972 and 2008, the percentage of conservatives increased from 55 to 78 percent while the percentage of moderates declined from 32 to only 17 percent and the percentage of liberals declined from 13 to only 5 percent. Thus, Republicans have gone from a predominantly conservative electoral base to an overwhelmingly conservative electoral base. Just as in the Congress, moderates have been reduced to a small minority within the party and liberals have almost disappeared.

Over the same time period, the Democratic electorate has also been transformed, although not quite as dramatically. Among Democratic voters, the percentage of liberals increased from 38 to 55 percent while the percentage of moderates declined from 38 to 32 percent, and the percentage of conservatives declined from 24 to 13 percent. Although conservative Democrats are not as rare as liberal Republicans, they are much less common than they were thirty or forty years ago. The Democratic electoral base has a decidedly liberal tilt today.

The political significance of the growing ideological gap between Democratic and Republican voters is heightened by the fact that the gap is greatest among the most politically engaged and therefore most influential members of the electorate, those with the highest levels of interest, knowledge, and involvement in the political process. This can be seen by comparing the average ideological locations of Democratic and Republican identifiers with different levels of involvement in presidential campaigns—those with no involvement beyond voting; those whose involvement included one activity beyond voting, most often trying to influence the vote of a friend or family member; and those whose involvement included at least two activities beyond voting, such as displaying a yard sign or bumper sticker, donating money to a party or candidate, or attending a campaign rally.

According to ANES data, the proportion of voters whose involvement in presidential campaigns extends beyond the basic act of voting is actually quite substantial, according to ANES data. On average, over the ten presidential elections between 1972 and 2008, about 52 percent of voters reported doing nothing beyond voting, 30 percent reported engaging in one campaign activity beyond voting, and 18 percent reported engaging in two or more campaign activities beyond voting. Moreover, the percentage of voters engaging in one or more activities beyond voting has increased in recent years. In the 2004 and 2008 elections, only 41 percent of voters reported doing nothing beyond voting while 35 percent reported engaging in one activity beyond voting, and 24 percent reported engaging in two or more activities beyond voting.

While the ideological divide between the parties increased among all types of voters, by far the largest ideological divide continues to be found among the most politically active segment of the American electorate. Politically active Democrats have been moving to the left while politically active Republicans have been moving even more rapidly to the right. Thus, between 1972 and 2008, the gap between politically active Democrats and Republicans on the ideological identification scale almost doubled, going from 1.5 to 2.8 units. The average position of politically active Democrats went from 3.2 to 2.8 units on the scale while the average position of politically active Republicans went from 4.7 to 5.6 units.

Again, to describe these trends in more concrete terms, conservatives increased from 60 percent of politically active Republicans in 1972 to 86 percent in 2008 while moderates fell from 24 percent in 1972 to only 10 percent in 2008 and liberals fell from 16 percent in 1972 to only 4 percent in 2008. Meanwhile, liberals increased from 57 percent of politically active Democrats in 1972 to 68 percent in 2008 while moderates fell from 30 percent in 1972 to 22 percent in 2008 and conservatives fell from 13 percent in 1972 to 10 percent in 2008. While there was already a large ideological divide between politically active Democrats and Republicans in 1972, that divide had widened considerably by 2008.

SORTING VERSUS POLARIZATION

How significant is the growing ideological divide between Democrats and Republicans in the American electorate? In order to answer this question, we must address an important challenge to mass polarization theory. Fiorina and his coauthors have argued that changes in Americans' ideological orientations over the past several decades have not actually been very large. They acknowledge that Americans today are better sorted into parties based on their ideological orientations than they were thirty or forty years ago, with liberals more likely to identify with the Democratic Party and conservatives more likely to identify with the Republican Party. However, they claim that even now the ideological and policy differences between Democrats and Republicans are not all that great and that Americans are no more polarized than they were thirty or forty years ago because the underlying distribution of ideological beliefs within the electorate has not changed.[7]

According to Fiorina, polarization, in contrast to sorting, involves a change in the shape of the distribution of the electorate on the liberal-conservative scale—a shift from a unimodal distribution, with most voters concentrated near the center, to a more even or bimodal distribution. In technical terms, sorting involves an increase in the distance between the mean locations of Democrats and Republicans on the ideology scale while polarization involves an increase in the standard deviation of the scale itself.

---

[7]Morris P. Fiorina with Samuel J. Abrams and Jeremy C. Pope, *Culture War? The Myth of a Polarized America*, 3rd ed. (New York: Longman, 2011), pp. 61–70. See also, Morris P. Fiorina and Matthew S. Levendusky, "Disconnected: The Political Class versus the People," in *Red and Blue Nation? Characteristics and Causes of America's Polarized Politics*, Vol. 1, ed. Pietro S. Nivola and David W. Brady (Washington, DC: Brookings Institution Press, 2006).

It is certainly true that supporters of the two major parties are much better sorted today than they were forty or fifty years ago in terms of their policy preferences and ideological orientations. This is evident from the fact that the correlation (Pearson's r) between party identification and ideological identification in the ANES surveys has increased steadily over the past four decades, rising from only .32 in 1972, which was the first year in which the ideological identification question was included in the survey, to .61 in 2008. This means that in terms of shared variance (r^2), the relationship between party identification and ideology was actually about four times stronger in 2008 than it was in 1972. And this is not an isolated trend: the correlations between party identification and a variety of specific issue questions have also strengthened over time. For example, the correlation between party identification and a seven-point scale measuring opinions on government responsibility for jobs and living standards rose from .19 in 1972, the first time both questions were included in the ANES survey, to .44 in 2008. In terms of shared variance, this means that the relationship between these two questions was actually more than five times stronger in 2008 than it was in 1972.

As Figure 3.5 illustrates (see Chapter 3 color insert), sorting could occur without any shift in the overall distribution of ideology within the public. This figure compares hypothetical distributions of Democratic and Republican identifiers on a liberal-conservative scale at two points in time. At time 1 (Figure 3.5a), there is no relationship between party and ideology—supporters of both parties are distributed identically on the ideology scale. By time 2 (Figure 3.5b), however, supporters of the two parties are perfectly sorted—all Democratic identifiers are on the liberal side of the scale and all Republican identifiers are on the conservative side of the scale. However, the shape of the distribution itself has not changed—the proportions of liberals, moderates, and conservatives are identical at time 2 and time 1.

Of course, even without a shift in the underlying distribution of the electorate on the ideology scale, partisan sorting would be a politically significant development, as one of Fiorina's coauthors has recently acknowledged.[8] The fact that Democrats and Republicans are now taking much more distinctive ideological positions has important implications for elections and representation. However, the claim that changes in Americans' political beliefs over the past several decades has been limited to sorting is simply not correct.

In the case of opinions about health care reform, we have already seen evidence in Chapter 1 that politically engaged members of the public, like political elites, were both highly sorted and highly polarized. There was a large gap between the preferences of politically engaged Democrats and Republicans on this issue, and the overall distribution of preferences was clearly bimodal with most voters located near the extremes of the scale and relatively few near the center. Evidence from national surveys conducted over the past several decades also shows very clearly that with regard to ideological beliefs, the process of partisan sorting has been accompanied by a substantial shift in the distribution of ideology within the public—a shift from a unimodal distribution toward a more even or bimodal distribution. While the distribution of opinion on the ideology scale in 2008 was not nearly as polarized as the distribution of opinion on the universal health care scale, it was substantially more polarized than in the past.

Figure 3.6 presents data on the relationship between partisan sorting and polarization on the seven-point ideological identification scale between 1972, the first time the ideology question was asked in the ANES survey, and 2008. Partisan sorting here is measured by the distance between the location of the average Democratic voter and the location of the average Republican voter on the ideology scale. Polarization, using the definition of Fiorina and his coauthors, is measured by the standard deviation of the ideology scale. An increase in the standard deviation of the scale means that the ideological distribution of the electorate is becoming less concentrated around the center and more evenly dispersed across the scale.

---

[8]Matthew Levendusky, *The Partisan Sort: How Liberals Became Democrats and Conservatives Became Republicans* (Chicago: University of Chicago Press, 2009).

FIGURE 3.6

Relationship between Partisan Sorting and Polarization among Voters in
American National Election Studies Surveys, 1972–2008

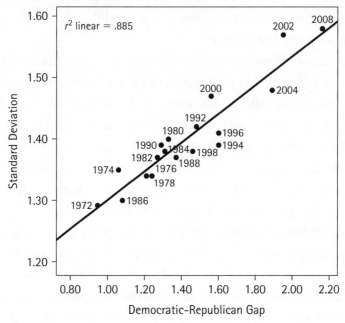

Source: American National Election Studies, 1952–2008

If the argument of Fiorina and his coauthors is correct, we should see an increase in sorting, the average distance between the parties on the ideology scale, over time but no increase in polarization, the standard deviation of the ideology scale. That would be consistent with the trend depicted in Figure 3.5 (see Chapter 3 color insert). However, the results displayed in Figure 3.6 present a very different picture. Both sorting and polarization have increased over time and these two trends have been very closely related. The lowest scores for both sorting and polarization occurred in the first election in this series, 1972, while the highest scores for both sorting and polarization occurred in the most recent election in this series, 2008. The correlation between ANES's measures of sorting and polarization across the eighteen elections for which ANES data are available is an extraordinarily strong .94.

A correlation coefficient of .94 means that ANES's measures of sorting and polarization have 88 percent of their variance in common.

That is, by any standard, a very strong relationship. Of course, correlation does not prove causation. Based on these results, we cannot say whether sorting has been driving polarization, polarization has been driving sorting, or some third factor has been driving both of these trends. But it is clear that sorting and polarization go together and that American voters, like members of Congress, have become both better sorted and more polarized over time. Moreover, the increases in both sorting and polarization within the electorate have been comparable to the increases in sorting and polarization within Congress. Between 1972 and 2008, the gap between the average Democratic voter and the average Republican voter on the seven-point liberal-conservative scale increased by 127 percent while the standard deviation of the scale increased by 24 percent. Over a similar period of time, between the 91st Congress (1969–70) and the 111th Congress (2009–10), the gap between the average Democratic member of the House of Representatives and the average Republican member of the House of Representatives on the DW-Nominate scale, a widely used measure of ideology, increased by 94 percent while the standard deviation of the scale increased by 28 percent.[9]

In substantive terms, the change in the shape of the distribution of the electorate on the ideology scale has been quite substantial. Between 1972 and 2008, voters placing themselves exactly in the middle of the seven-point scale fell from 35 percent of the electorate to 27 percent and those placing themselves within one unit of the center fell from 36 percent of the electorate to 27 percent. At the same time, voters placing themselves within one unit of the two extremes of the scale rose from 29 percent of the electorate to 46 percent. These results indicate that a much larger proportion of voters today have a strong ideological identification. Moreover, there is little doubt that the change would be even more dramatic if we had data on the electorate of the 1950s and 1960s since the process of ideological realignment was already well underway by 1972.

---

[9]An explanation of the DW-Nominate scale and data on members of Congress can be found at http://voteview.com/dwnomin.htm. See also Keith T. Poole and Howard L. Rosenthal, *Ideology and Congress*, 2nd ed. (New York: Transaction Book, 2007).

The change in the distribution of politically active voters on the ideology scale has been even greater than the change in the overall electorate. Among those engaging in two or more campaign activities beyond voting, a group that made up just over a fifth of the electorate in 1972 and a quarter of the electorate in 2008, those placing themselves exactly in the middle of the seven-point liberal-conservative scale fell from 28 percent of active voters in 1972 to only 19 percent in 2008 and those placing themselves within one unit of the center fell from 35 percent of active voters in 1972 to 23 percent in 2008. At the same time, those placing themselves within one unit of either end of the scale rose from 37 percent of active voters in 1972 to 58 percent in 2008. Thus, by 2008 strong liberals and conservatives (those located at 1, 2, 6, and 7 on the scale) outnumbered moderates (those located at 4) by a better than three-to-one margin among the most politically active members of the electorate.

Issue Constraint and Polarization

Ideological identification provides only one way of evaluating trends in polarization. Another approach involves looking at trends in constraint or consistency in opinions across different issues. In his groundbreaking work on belief systems in mass publics, Philip Converse argued that constraint was a key indicator of ideological thinking because if members of the public possess coherent ideologies, those ideologies should influence their responses to a variety of specific issues. What Converse found, however, was very little evidence of constraint in the American public of the 1950s. The correlations between responses to different issue questions, even those within a specific policy domain such as domestic social welfare policy, were very low. In contrast, the correlations between responses to different issue questions were much stronger among members of the political elite—in this case, candidates for Congress. Therefore, Converse concluded that ideological thinking was much more prevalent among political elites than among the public in the 1950s.[10]

---

[10]Converse, "The Nature of Belief Systems in Mass Publics."

The degree of constraint in opinions across issues is directly related to the level of polarization within the public. That is because higher constraint means that a larger proportion of the public hold consistently liberal or consistently conservative views across issues and a smaller proportion hold centrist or mixed views. This is very similar to the way in which we typically evaluate polarization among members of Congress except that for members of Congress we measure consistency by roll call votes rather than survey responses.[11]

Unfortunately, it is difficult to evaluate trends in issue constraint over time within the American public because very few issue questions have been included consistently in public opinion surveys for long enough to make meaningful comparisons over time possible. However, we do have data on constraint across five questions measuring support for activist government that were included in ANES surveys in every presidential election year between 1984 and 2008. While twenty-four years is not as long a time period as we would like to include in our analysis, it does cover most of the recent era of rising partisan polarization.

The five questions that have been included in ANES surveys since 1984 ask about ideological identification, government aid to blacks, government versus individual responsibility for jobs and living standards, government versus private responsibility for health insurance, and the tradeoff between government services and taxes. All of these questions tap into beliefs about the role of government in society and, therefore, it is not surprising that responses to them are somewhat related. However, the evidence from the ANES shows that the degree of consistency of voters' responses to these five questions has increased considerably over time. Between 1984 and 2008, the average correlation (Pearson's r) across these five issues increased from a modest .31 to a much stronger .47. In technical

---

[11]One key difference is that members of Congress are provided with information by party leaders about the position of their party on controversial issues. Respondents in public opinions surveys receive no such information. If they did, one might well expect to find greater consistency in their responses.

terms, this means that the average amount of shared variance between the items more than doubled, going from less than 10 percent to more than 22 percent.

The consequences of this increase in constraint for polarization can be seen very clearly when we examine the changing distribution of opinions on a governmental activism scale that combines the responses of voters to these five questions. The scale has a range from 0 percent (the most liberal response to all five questions) to 100 percent (the most conservative response to all five questions). In order to display the distribution of opinions on the scale, the percentage scores were recoded into six categories: very liberal (0 to 16 percent), liberal (17 to 33 percent), slightly liberal (34 to 50 percent), slightly conservative (51 to 66 percent), conservative (67 to 83 percent), and very conservative (84 to 100 percent).

Location on this recoded scale had a very strong relationship with presidential voting decisions, indicating that the scale is a valid measure of political ideology. Over the seven presidential elections between 1984 and 2008, Democratic presidential candidates received 98 percent of the major party vote among those classified as "very liberal," 91 percent of the vote among those classified as "liberal," 71 percent of the vote among those classified as "slightly liberal," 38 percent of the vote among those classified as "slightly conservative," 12 percent of the vote among those classified as "conservative," and 4 percent of the vote among those classified as "very conservative."

As was the case with the ideological identification question, the evidence with regard to the governmental activism scale shows that over time there was a substantial increase in both the distance between the average Democratic and Republican voter and the standard deviation of the scores on the scale. The distance between the scores of the average Democratic and Republican voter on the full scale increased from 20 percentage points in 1984 to 33 percentage points in 2008 while the standard deviation of the scale increased from 17 percentage points in 1984 to 23 percentage points in 2008.

The significance of these changes in the distribution of scores on the governmental activism scale is readily apparent in Figure 3.7,

FIGURE 3.7
Distribution of Voters on Governmental Activism Scale in 1984 and 2008

a.

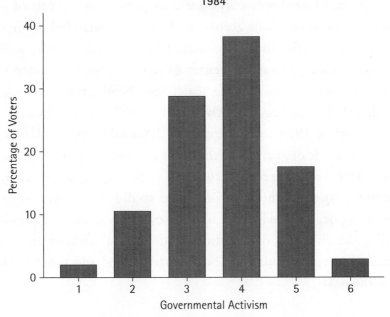

1984

1. Very liberal 2. Liberal 3. Slightly liberal 4. Slightly conservative
5. Conservative 6. Very conservative

b.

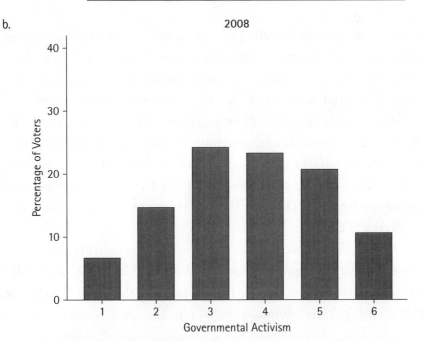

2008

Source: American National Election Studies, 1952–2008

which compares the distribution of scores on the recoded version of the scale in 1984 with the distribution of scores on the same recoded scale in 2008. Over this twenty-four-year period, as a result of growing consistency in opinions across the five issues included in the scale, the shape of the distribution changed fairly dramatically, with far fewer voters located near the center of the scale and far more voters located near the extremes of the scale. Specifically, those classified as only "slightly liberal" or "slightly conservative" declined from 67 percent of voters in 1984 to 48 percent in 2008 while those classified as further to the left or further to the right increased from 33 percent of voters in 1984 to 52 percent in 2008. So as the gap between supporters of the two parties on the scale increased so did the dispersion of voters on the scale. This evidence, like the evidence examined previously regarding the changing distribution of ideological identification, demonstrates that voters today are both better sorted and more polarized than in the past.

POLITICAL ENGAGEMENT, CONSTRAINT, AND POLARIZATION: EVIDENCE FROM 2010

We have seen that partisan sorting and polarization have both increased within the U.S. electorate over the past several decades and that these two trends are directly related. Partisan sorting and polarization are also directly related within the electorate when we compare groups with different levels of political engagement. At any given time, the most interested, informed, and active members of the public are both the best sorted by party and most polarized. This can be seen very clearly from data from a recent survey of the U.S. voting age population sponsored by the ANES, the 2010 Evaluations of Government and Society Survey (EGSS).

The EGSS included a series of questions asking respondents about their opinions on nine major policy issues: repeal of the "don't ask, don't tell" policy toward gays serving openly in the military, the 2010 health care reform law, the 2009 economic stimulus bill, the 2009 financial reform law, expansion of the state children's health insurance program, raising taxes on upper income households, federal funding for stem cell research, and federal support for clean energy development. These eight items along with the standard ideological identification question were combined to form a nine-item, liberal-conservative policy scale with scores ranging from one (consistently liberal) to twelve (consistently conservative).

The EGSS also included a series of questions asking respondents about their interest in politics, knowledge of current political leaders, frequency of political discussions with family members and neighbors, and participation in political activities. These questions were combined to form a ten-item political engagement scale. I then grouped respondents into two broad categories—those whose scores placed them in the upper half of the political engagement scale and those whose scores placed them in the lower half.

The data from the 2010 EGSS show that those who were more engaged in politics were both far better sorted and much more polarized than those who were less engaged. Based on the raw scores on the ideology scale, the gap between the average Democratic identifier and the average Republican identifier was 2.0 units among those who scored in the lower half of the political engagement scale compared with 6.0 units among those who scored in the upper half. At the same time, the standard deviation of the ideology scale was only 2.4 units among the less engaged half of the sample compared with 3.8 units among those in the more engaged half of the sample.

The significance of these differences in partisan sorting and polarization is readily apparent in Figure 3.8 (see Chapter 3 color insert), which compares the distributions of ideology by party identification for less politically engaged and more politically engaged respondents. The scale here has been collapsed from its original twelve categories into five categories: very liberal, liberal, moderate, conservative, and very conservative. In the low engagement group, most of the respondents are clustered around the modal position on the scale and the difference between party supporters is modest, with Republicans only slightly more conservative than Democrats. In contrast, in the high engagement group most of the respondents are clustered toward the left and right poles of the scale and the difference between party supporters is very large, with Republicans concentrated heavily at the conservative end of the scale and Democrats concentrated heavily at the liberal end of the scale.

POLARIZED POSITIONS OR POLARIZED CHOICES?

There is one additional attack on mass polarization theory that remains to be discussed. Fiorina and his coauthors have argued that what appear to be deep divisions within the American public over policy issues or political leaders reflect the polarized choices that the parties are presenting to the public rather than polarized positions or preferences within the public.[12]

The problem confronting critics of mass polarization is the fact that over time the public's evaluations of political leaders and their policies have become increasingly divided along party lines. For example, according to data from ANES surveys, in the fall of 1972, 88 percent of Republicans and 50 percent of Democrats approved of the job that Richard Nixon was doing as president—a gap of 38 percentage points; in the fall of 2004, however, 90 percent of Republicans and only 19 percent of Democrats approved of the job that George W. Bush was doing as president—a gap of 71 percentage points. And the situation hasn't changed much under Barack Obama. According to the Gallup Poll, between June 13 and July 17 of 2011, Obama's approval rating averaged 80 percent among Democrats compared with 13 percent among Republicans, a gap of 67 percentage points.

The explanation for the growing partisan divide in opinions of presidential performance, according to Fiorina and his coauthors, is not that the American public has become more polarized in its political outlook but that more recent political leaders have presented the public with more polarized choices, thereby forcing Americans to take sides. In other

---

[12]Fiorina with Abrams and Pope, *Culture War?*, pp. 25–32.

words, the fact that political leaders are presenting the public with a more polarized stimulus is what is producing a more polarized response. In the preceding examples, the argument is that George W. Bush in 2004 and Barack Obama in 2011 were inherently more polarizing figures than Richard Nixon in 1972.

The problem with this argument is that a polarized stimulus alone cannot produce a polarized response from the public. It takes both a polarized stimulus and a public with polarized preferences to produce a polarized response by the public. If voters were all centrists, they would be expected to respond very similarly to a strongly conservative stimulus such as George W. Bush or to a strongly liberal stimulus like Barack Obama rather than being divided between those having a strongly positive reaction and those having a strongly negative reaction.

Similarly, according to this argument, a choice between polarized candidates like George W. Bush and John Kerry in the 2004 presidential election should have produced an overwhelmingly neutral or indifferent response from a centrist public. But this was not what happened. The response to the choice between Bush and Kerry was itself highly polarized. The large majority of voters expressed a strong preference for one candidate or the other. Very few were neutral. In fact, 50 percent of voters rated their preferred candidate at least 50 degrees higher than the opposing candidate on the feeling thermometer scale—the largest proportion of voters expressing that strong a preference in any presidential election since the ANES first introduced the feeling thermometer scale in 1968. That was because liberals strongly preferred Kerry while conservatives strongly preferred Bush. Fifty-five percent of liberals preferred Kerry by at least 50 degrees while 48 percent of conservatives preferred Bush by at least 50 degrees. The polarized response was a reflection of a polarized electorate, not just polarized choices.

The polarized choices versus polarized positions argument is based on the assumption that the large majority of American voters are located in the middle of the ideological spectrum while the parties and candidates, in Fiorina's terms, "hang out at the extremes." And at first glance there appears to be some evidence for this claim. Figure 3.9a

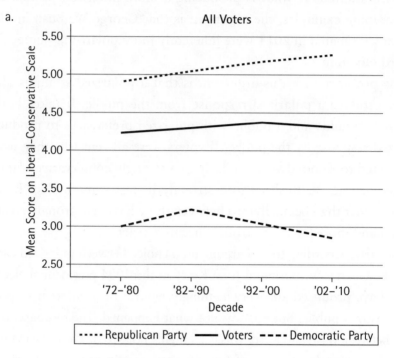

FIGURE 3.9

Average Positions of Voters and Parties on Liberal–Conservative Scale by Decade

a. All Voters

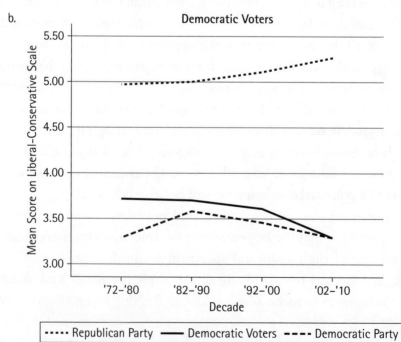

b. Democratic Voters

FIGURE 3.9 *(Continued)*

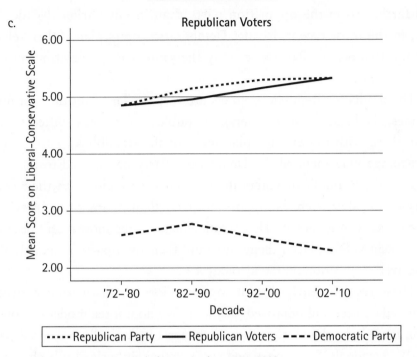

c. **Republican Voters**

Source: American National Election Studies, 1952–2008

displays the trends in the average positions where voters placed themselves and the two major parties on the seven-point liberal-conservative
scale between the 1970s and the 2000s. This graph appears to show that
over the past four decades the average voter has remained slightly to
the right-of-center on the liberal-conservative scale while the Democratic
Party has moved to the left and the Republican Party has moved to the
right. As a result, it appears that the gap between the average voter and
both parties has been growing.

But this appearance of a growing gap between the average voter
and both parties is an illusion based on lumping supporters of the two
parties together into one group. When we separate Democratic voters
from Republican voters, with leaning independents included with the
party they lean toward, we get a very different picture, as Figures 3.9b
and 3.9c clearly demonstrate. In Figure 3.9b, we see that Democratic

voters in the 2000s perceived themselves to be closer to their own party and farther from the opposition party than in any earlier decade. In fact, in the most recent decade, Democratic voters placed themselves and the Democratic Party at exactly the same average position on the ideology scale.

The results for Republican voters are very similar. Over the past four decades, the location of the average Republican voter has shifted to the right along with the average placement of the Republican Party while the average placement of the Democratic Party has shifted to the left. As a result, Republican voters in the 2000s were closer to their own party and farther from the opposition party than in any of the previous three decades. And as with Democratic voters, in the most recent decade, Republican voters placed themselves and their own party at exactly the same average position on the ideology scale.

These results clearly do not support Fiorina's distinction between polarized choices and polarized positions. We do not see moderate voters being forced to reluctantly choose between ideologically polarized parties. We see ideologically polarized voters rather enthusiastically choosing between ideologically polarized parties. It is precisely this combination of polarized choices and polarized positions that explains the deep partisan divide in evaluations of political leaders and their policies in the contemporary American electorate.

Chapter Summary

Since the 1950s, the American party system has undergone an ideological realignment. That realignment has transformed the electoral bases of the two major parties. Democrats today are more likely to identify themselves as liberals and take more consistently liberal positions on issues than at any time in recent history while Republicans today are more likely to identify themselves as conservatives and take more consistently conservative positions than at any time in recent history. Not only are supporters of the two parties more deeply divided in terms of ideology and policy than at any time in recent history, but the sharpest divisions are found among the most interested, informed, and active supporters of the parties. We will see in Chapter 4 that the party divide now extends beyond the traditional issues of governmental activism to cultural issues such as abortion and gay rights that reflect fundamental moral values and religious beliefs.

CHAPTER 4

The Cultural Divide

The simple truth is that there is no culture war in the United States—no battle
for the soul of America rages, at least none that most Americans are aware of.
—Morris P. Fiorina[1]

Apparently, nobody told the new Republican majority in the U.S.
House of Representatives that the culture war had been cancelled. On
February 18, 2011, in one of its first major acts, the House voted 240 to
185 to cut off all federal funding of Planned Parenthood, an organization
that provides family planning services, including abortions, for low income
women. The amount of money involved was relatively small, no federal
funds were being used to pay for abortions and abortions accounted for only
a small fraction of the organization's family planning services. Nevertheless,
defunding Planned Parenthood was a top priority of Republican leaders
because it allowed them to reward a group of supporters who were critical
to the GOP's 2010 midterm election gains—religious conservatives.

The House vote to defund Planned Parenthood almost perfectly
followed party lines. Republicans voted 230 to 10 in favor of cutting off
funding while Democrats voted 178 to 7 against cutting off funding.[2] And

---

[1]Morris P. Fiorina with Samuel J. Abrams and Jeremy C. Pope, *Culture War? The Myth of a Polarized America*, 3rd ed. (New York: Longman, 2011), p. 8.

[2]Erik Eckholm, "Planned Parenthood Funding Is Caught in Budget Dispute," *New York Times* (February 18, 2011): A16.

the GOP attack on Planned Parenthood did not stop there. Following the House vote, several Republican-controlled state legislatures quickly moved to cut off state funding of Planned Parenthood. As with the U.S. House of Representatives, the votes to cut off funding in the states followed party lines, with Republicans voting overwhelmingly in favor of cutting off funding and Democrats voting overwhelmingly against cutting off funding.[3]

There may not be a battle raging for the soul of America, but there clearly is a battle raging for the hearts and minds of American voters, and cultural issues such as abortion have become major weapons in that battle. The reason that battle continues to rage is because there is a deep cultural divide in the American electorate.

The cultural divide was very evident in the results of the 2008 presidential election despite the fact that the election took place in the midst of a major economic crisis and neither major party candidate focused much attention on cultural issues during the campaign. One of the strongest predictors of candidate choice among white voters in 2008 was frequency of church attendance.[4] The data from the 2008 national exit poll displayed in Figure 4.1 show that the more time white voters reported spending in church, the more likely they were to cast a Republican ballot. Among whites who never attended religious services, less than 40 percent voted for the Republican presidential candidate, but among those who attended religious services more than once a week, almost 80 percent voted for the Republican candidate.

That candidate, John McCain, was no favorite of religious conservatives. He had received little support in the Republican primaries from born-again and evangelical voters, many of whom preferred former Arkansas governor Mike Huckabee, an ordained Baptist minister. McCain's decision to choose little-known Alaska governor Sarah Palin

---

[3]See Kaiser Health News, "States Are Battleground for Planned Parenthood Funding, Abortion Issues," *Kaiser Health News Daily Report* (May 4, 2011): http://www.kaiserhealthnews.org/daily-reports/2011/may/04/planned-parenthood-abortion.aspx.

[4]For the most part, the cultural divide in American politics involves white voters. Nonwhites, including African-Americans and Latinos, are also divided on cultural issues but those divisions generally have little or no relevance to their party affiliations or candidate choices. The evidence presented in this chapter will, therefore, focus mainly on the cultural divide among white Americans.

FIGURE 4.1

2008 Presidential Vote of Whites by Church Attendance

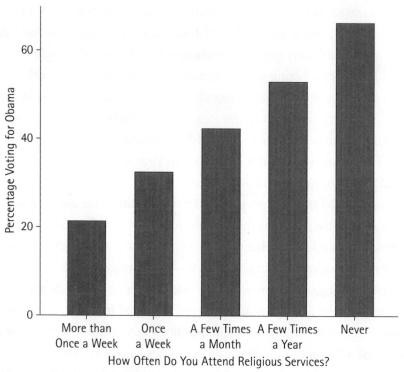

How Often Do You Attend Religious Services?

Source: 2008 National Exit Poll

as his running mate was viewed by many political commentators as an attempt to generate enthusiasm for the GOP ticket among religious conservatives.[5] Hoping to take advantage of McCain's weakness among this group, Democratic nominee Barack Obama made a concerted effort during the 2008 campaign to stress his Christian beliefs and to reach out to religious voters. It made no difference. Obama fared little better among religious whites than the Democrats' 2004 nominee, John Kerry.

[5]For an informative and entertaining account of the 2008 nomination and general election campaigns, see John Heilemann and Mark Halperin, *Game Change: Obama and the Clintons, McCain and Palin, and the Race of a Lifetime* (New York: Harper, 2010). See also Dan Balz and Haynes Johnson, *The Battle for America 2008: The Story of an Extraordinary Election* (New York: Viking, 2009). Scholarly perspectives on the 2008 election can be found in Larry J. Sabato, ed., *The Year of Obama: How Barack Obama Won the White House* (New York: Longman, 2010).

Kerry had received 21 percent of the vote among white born-again and evangelical Christians. Obama received 24 percent.

Religiosity is now a powerful predictor of party identification and candidate preference among white voters in the United States—more powerful in many elections than characteristics traditionally associated with party affiliation and voting behavior such as social class and union membership.[6] Thus, data from the 2008 national exit poll show that among white voters the impact of church attendance on candidate choice was much stronger than the impact of either family income or union membership. The difference in support for Obama between whites who attended church more than once a week and those who never attended church was a stunning 45 percentage points. In contrast, the difference in support for Obama between whites with family incomes below $30,000 and those with family incomes above $150,000 was a meager 6 percentage points. And despite the strong support that he received from organized labor in the general election, the difference in support for Obama between whites in union households and those in nonunion households was only 9 percentage points.

The data in Table 4.1 show that regardless of income or household union membership, religious whites voted overwhelmingly for the Republican presidential candidate in 2008. Thus, whites with family incomes below $50,000 who attended religious services more than once a week voted for John McCain over Barack Obama by better than a two-to-one margin. And despite the strong support of union leaders for the Democratic ticket, whites from union households who attended religious services more than once a week voted for McCain over Obama by close to a three-to-one margin.

On the other hand, regardless of income or household union membership, secular whites voted overwhelmingly for the Democratic presidential candidate in 2008. Whites with family incomes above $100,000 who never attended religious services voted for Obama over McCain by better than a two-to-one margin and whites from nonunion households who

---

[6]For an exploration of the changing role of religion in American life and the relationship between religious beliefs and practices and political attitudes, see Robert D. Putnam and David E. Campbell, *American Grace: How Religion Divides and Unites Us* (New York: Simon & Schuster, 2010).

TABLE 4.1

Percentage of Whites Voting for Obama in 2008 by Church Attendance, Family Income, and Union Membership

	MORE THAN WEEKLY	ONCE A WEEK	FEW TIMES A MONTH	FEW TIMES A YEAR	NEVER
ALL VOTERS	21	32	42	53	66
INCOME					
UNDER 50,000	30	42	46	56	64
50–100,000	17	22	49	46	66
OVER 100,000	11	35	32	55	70
HOUSEHOLD					
UNION	26	38	46	60	82
NONUNION	20	31	41	51	63

Source: 2008 national exit poll

never attended religious services voted for Obama over McCain by better than a three-to-two margin.

The deep partisan divide between religious and nonreligious whites is a relatively recent development in American politics. In the years following World War II, the most significant religious divide among white voters in the United States was that between Protestants and Catholics. White Catholics were strongly Democratic while white Protestants outside of the South were almost as strongly Republican. In the 1960 presidential election, for example, according to data from the American National Election Study (ANES) survey, 82 percent of white Catholics voted for Democrat John F. Kennedy while 71 percent of white Protestants in the North voted for Republican Richard M. Nixon.

Since the 1960s, the partisan divide between white Catholics and Protestants has gradually diminished as a result of the ideological realignment of the American party system. Conservative Catholics have gravitated toward the Republican Party while liberal Protestants have moved into the Democratic camp. By 2008, according to the ANES survey, the 46 percent of white Catholics who voted for Barack Obama was almost identical to the 45 percent of northern white Protestants who voted for

Obama. However, as the Catholic-Protestant split has diminished, a new religious divide has emerged among white voters—a divide between the religious and the nonreligious.

Figure 4.2 displays the trend in party identification among white voters between the 1960s and the first decade of the twenty-first century based on frequency of church attendance. Voters were classified as "observant" if they reported attending religious services every week or almost every week and as "nonobservant" if they reported attending religious services only a few times a year or never. On average, about 40 percent of white voters fell into each of these two categories. About 20 percent of white voters who reported attending religious services "a few times a month" are left out of the graph. Their party identification generally falls right in the middle of the "observant" and "nonobservant" groups.

The data in Figure 4.2 show that between the 1960s and the 1980s Democratic identification (which includes independents leaning toward

FIGURE 4.2

Trend in Democratic Identification among White Voters by Church Attendance

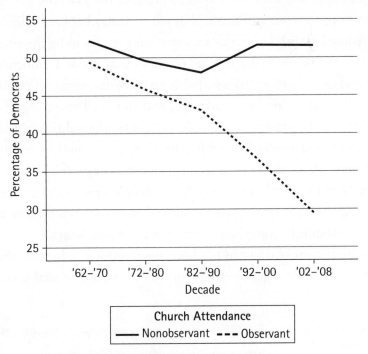

Source: American National Election Studies, 1952–2008

the Democratic Party) declined among both observant and nonobservant whites, with the gap between the two groups growing only slightly. Since then, however, the gap has widened considerably due mainly to a sharp drop in Democratic identification among observant whites. During this more recent period, Democratic identification has increased modestly among nonobservant whites. As a result, by the 2000s, the religious divide among white voters had reached an all-time high. Slightly over 50 percent of nonobservant white voters identified with or leaned toward the Democratic Party compared with less than 30 percent of observant white voters. To put this in perspective, the twenty-two-point gap in Democratic identification between observant and nonobservant whites was considerably larger than either the thirteen-point marriage gap or the seven-point gender gap among white voters.

EXPLAINING THE RELIGIOUS DIVIDE: THE RISE OF ABORTION AS A POLITICAL ISSUE

What has happened since the 1970s to produce the yawning gap in party identification and voting behavior that we see today between religious and secular white voters? The major explanation appears to be the emergence during this time period of a new set of issues that divide Democratic candidates and officeholders from Republican candidates and officeholders—issues such as abortion, gay marriage, and stem cell research. These are issues that, for the most part, were simply not on the political agenda during the 1950s and 1960s. They differ from the traditional issues involving the size and role of the federal government that have divided the parties since the New Deal in that they tap into voters' moral values and religious beliefs. And for that reason, these cultural issues are often more divisive and more difficult to compromise on than economic issues.[7]

One of the most divisive of these new cultural issues is abortion. We can trace the emergence of abortion as a major national issue in the

[7]See John Kenneth White, *The Values Divide: American Politics and Culture in Transition* (New York: Chatham House, 2003).

United States to the Supreme Court's 1973 *Roe v. Wade* decision, which essentially legalized abortion during the first trimester of pregnancy.[8] Even after *Roe v. Wade*, however, it took time for abortion to develop into a partisan issue. Initially, there was little reaction to the decision from national political leaders. Opposition to *Roe v. Wade* was concentrated mainly among certain religious leaders, especially Roman Catholic clergy. Among the public, as well, opinions on abortion divided along religious lines rather than partisan lines. Religious voters in both parties tended to oppose legalized abortion while nonreligious voters in both parties tended to support a woman's right to choose whether to continue or terminate a pregnancy.

It was not until Ronald Reagan's 1980 presidential campaign that the issue of abortion clearly began to divide Democrats from Republicans. Although he had never expressed much interest in the issue of abortion during his years as Governor of California, by 1980 Reagan and his advisors saw abortion as a potential wedge issue—one that could divide Democrats and attract religious conservatives, whether Protestant or Catholic, into the Republican camp.[9] The Republican Party's 1980 platform included a plank strongly opposing legalized abortion and endorsing a constitutional amendment to overturn *Roe v. Wade*.[10]

By the late 1980s and 1990s, the party divide on the issue of abortion was clear, with Republican leaders increasingly taking the side of religious conservatives in supporting restrictions on access to abortion if not an outright ban and Democratic leaders increasingly taking the side of feminist organizations in defending *Roe v. Wade* and women's access to legal abortion. Today, it is difficult to find prominent Republican politicians who support legalized abortion or prominent Democratic politicians who

---

[8]For an in-depth examination of the emergence of abortion as a national issue and its impact on U.S. politics, see Barbara H. Craig and David M. O'Brien, *Abortion and American Politics* (New York: Chatham House, 1993). See also Karen O'Connor, *No Neutral Ground: Abortion Politics in an Age of Absolutes* (Boulder, CO: Westview Press, 1996).

[9]See Andrew E. Busch, *Reagan's Victory: The 1980 Presidential Election and the Rise of the Right* (Lawrence: University Press of Kansas, 2005).

[10]The full text of the 1980 Republican platform can be found on the Web site of the American Presidency Project: http://www.presidency.ucsb.edu/ws/index.php?pid=25844#axzz1TzeBNGvG.

oppose it. Certainly, no candidate seeking the Republican or Democratic presidential nomination in the twenty-first century could take a position contrary to the now-established position of his or her party on abortion and hope to be successful. A pro-choice Republican would have no chance of winning the Republican nomination for president and a pro-life Democrat would have no chance of winning the Democratic nomination for president. Indeed, only a handful of pro-choice Republicans and pro-life Democrats remain in Congress.

But the partisan divide on abortion is by no means limited to elected officials, candidates, and activists. It is now firmly entrenched among the parties' rank-and-file supporters, as the data displayed in Figure 4.3 make clear. This graph shows the trend in party identification among white voters with opposing positions on the issue of abortion based on data

FIGURE 4.3
Trend in Democratic Identification among White Voters by Abortion Attitude

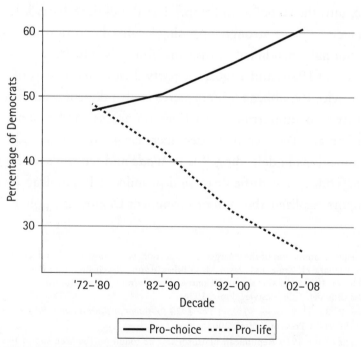

Source: American National Election Studies, 1952–2008

from ANES surveys conducted over four decades. Voters were classified as "pro-life" if they indicated that abortion should always be illegal or should be legal only in cases involving rape, incest, or danger to the life of the mother. Those are the sorts of relatively rare exceptions that are often supported by Republican candidates and elected officials, though even those exceptions have not been included in the language of the Republican Party's national platform in recent presidential elections. On the other side, voters were classified as "pro-choice" if they indicated that "a woman should always be able to have an abortion as a matter of personal choice."

The ANES has been using this particular question since 1980 to measure opinions on the issue of abortion. Over this time period, the distribution of opinion on this issue has fluctuated within a fairly narrow range. On average, 41 percent of voters were classified as "pro-choice" and 42 percent were classified as "pro-life." An average of 17 percent of voters who indicated that they supported legalized abortion "for reasons other than rape, incest, or danger to the woman's life, but only after the need for the abortion has been clearly established" were placed in a middle category. That category is excluded from Figure 4.3. In terms of party identification, this group generally falls right in the middle of the pro-life and pro-choice groups.

Of course, there are many ways to measure opinions on abortion policy. In using the results of the ANES question to divide voters into two opposing camps, we are simplifying a more complex set of opinions. As Fiorina and his coauthors have correctly pointed out, most Americans have ambivalent feelings about abortion.[11] No doubt many of America's pro-choice voters would support some limited restrictions on access to abortion and many of America's pro-life voters would permit abortions to take place under some extreme circumstances. Despite their ambivalent feelings, however, the large majority of voters in the United States clearly fall into one of two opposing camps on the fundamental question

---

[11]Fiorina with Abrams and Pope, *Culture War? The Myth of a Polarized America*, chapter 5.

of whether abortion should remain legal under the large majority of circumstances, as *Roe v. Wade* provides, or whether it should be banned under the large majority of circumstances. And that is the division that matters politically. Among white voters in the United States today, the large majority of those on the pro-choice side of that divide are Democrats while the large majority of those on the pro-life side of that divide are Republicans.

The data in Figure 4.3 show that over the past four decades the party divide on the issue of abortion has steadily widened. Initially there was no difference in party identification between white voters on opposite sides of the abortion issue. Pro-life voters were just as likely to be Democrats as pro-choice voters. By the 2000s, however, there was a deep partisan divide between pro-life and pro-choice voters. In 2008, for example, 62 percent of pro-choice voters identified with or leaned toward the Democratic Party compared with only 24 percent of pro-life voters. This divide was also reflected in the presidential candidate choices of the two groups. Sixty-five percent of pro-choice whites voted for Barack Obama while 78 percent of pro-life whites voted for John McCain.

But the issue of abortion was not equally divisive among all voters in 2008. This can be seen in Table 4.2, which compares the size of the partisan divide on abortion among white voters based on the importance that these voters accorded the issue of abortion and their level of involvement in the 2008 campaign. In terms of issue importance, voters who considered abortion to be a "very important" or "extremely important" issue were placed in the "more important" category while those who considered it only "somewhat important," "not very important," or "not at all important" were placed in the "less important" category. Just under half of white voters rated the issue of abortion as either "very important" or "extremely important."

With regard to campaign involvement, those who engaged in no activities beyond voting were placed in the low involvement group, those who engaged in one activity beyond voting were placed in the moderate involvement group, and those who engaged in two or more activities

TABLE 4.2
The Party Divide on Abortion in 2008: Percentage of Democratic Identifiers by Abortion Opinion among White Voters

	PRO-CHOICE	PRO-LIFE	DIFFERENCE
ALL VOTERS	62	24	38
ABORTION IMPORTANCE			
LESS IMPORTANT	55	35	20
MORE IMPORTANT	69	16	53
CAMPAIGN INVOLVEMENT			
LOW	53	36	17
MODERATE	62	20	42
HIGH	75	8	67

Source: 2008 American National Election Study

beyond voting were placed in the high involvement group. Thirty-seven percent of white voters were in the low involvement group, 37 percent were in the moderate involvement group, and 26 percent were in the high involvement group.

The results in Table 4.2 show that the partisan divide on abortion was much larger among white voters who considered abortion an important issue than among those who did not consider it an important issue and much larger among those who were politically active than among those who were not politically active. And the deepest partisan divide on abortion was found among those voters who cared about the issue and were also politically active. Among active Democrats who cared about abortion, 88 percent were pro-choice. Among active Republicans who cared about abortion, 84 percent were pro-life.

Given these divisions within the electorate, it is hardly surprising that officeholders and candidates are also deeply divided on this issue, with Democrats overwhelmingly on the pro-choice side and Republicans overwhelmingly on the pro-life side. There is no "disconnect" between politicians and voters on this issue. Democratic officeholders and candidates are accurately reflecting the pro-choice views of their party's active supporters while Republican officeholders and candidates are accurately reflecting the views of their party's active supporters.

CULTURAL ISSUES IN 2008:
ABORTION AND GAY RIGHTS

Abortion is not the only cultural issue dividing American voters. Opinions on abortion are closely related to opinions on a number of other issues that involve deeply held moral and religious beliefs, especially issues concerning the rights of gays and lesbians in American society. There is considerable evidence that attitudes on issues involving gays and lesbians are changing fairly rapidly in the United States. Younger Americans are generally much more accepting of homosexuality than older Americans and much more likely to support policies protecting the rights of gays and lesbians including the right to marry. There has also been a substantial increase since the 1990s in the proportion of American adults who favor allowing gays and lesbians to serve openly in the military and who support same sex marriage. In May 2011, the Gallup Poll reported that for the first time a majority of Americans supported legalizing marriage between same sex couples.[12]

Given these trends, it is entirely possible that at some time in the future, civil rights for gays and lesbians will no longer divide Americans along party lines. But that time is not yet here. In fact, even as overall support for homosexual rights has increased in recent years, the party divide on these issues appears to have widened. Support for same sex marriage and for other policies protecting the rights of gays and lesbians has been growing much more rapidly among Democrats than among Republicans. In the May 2011 Gallup Poll, for example, same sex marriage was supported by 69 percent of Democratic identifiers but by only 28 percent of Republican identifiers. This forty-one-point gap between Democrats and Republicans was substantially larger than the twenty-eight-point gap in a

---

[12]Frank Newport, "For First Time, Majority of Americans Favor Legal Gay Marriage," *Gallup Poll*: http://www.gallup.com/poll/147662/First-Time-Majority-Americans-Favor-Legal-Gay-Marriage.aspx.

FIGURE 4.4

Party Divide on Cultural Issues among Whites in 2008
by Campaign Involvement

a.

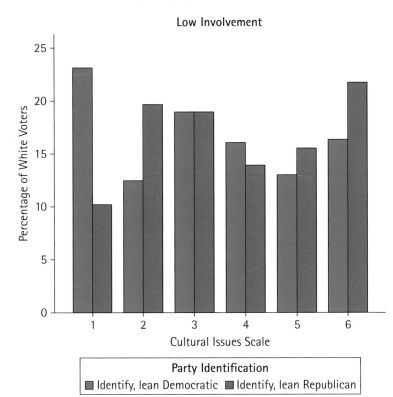

Low Involvement

FIGURE 4.4 (*Continued*)

b.

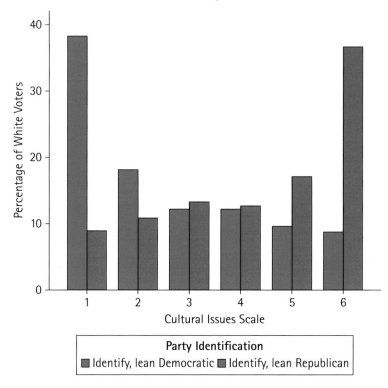

Moderate to High Involvement

Party Identification
Identify, lean Democratic Identify, lean Republican

1. Very liberal 2. Liberal 3. Leaning liberal 4. Leaning conservative
5. Conservative 6. Very conservative

Source: 2008 American National Election Study

2010 Gallup Poll. So while antigay sentiment appears to be diminishing within the American electorate, gay rights continue to be a divisive issue in the United States. And that was certainly the case in the 2008 presidential election.

In 2008, the ANES for the first time incorporated questions on gay rights, including one on same sex marriage and one on adoption by gay and lesbian couples. The data displayed in Table 4.3 show that opinions on gay marriage and adoption, like opinions on abortion, were closely related to frequency of religious observance among white voters. The more often white voters attended church, the less likely they were to favor giving

TABLE 4.3
Cultural Attitudes of White Voters in 2008 by Religious Observance

	OBSERVANT (%)	NONOBSERVANT (%)
ABORTION		
PRO-CHOICE	21	53
MIXED	15	18
PRO-LIFE	64	29
GAY MARRIAGE		
PRO-MARRIAGE	17	50
CIVIL UNIONS	28	28
NEITHER	55	22
GAY ADOPTION		
FAVOR	29	66
OPPOSE	71	34
CULTURAL ISSUES SCALE		
VERY LIBERAL	7	33
LIBERAL	9	17
SLIGHTLY LIBERAL	8	15
SLIGHTLY CONSERVATIVE	14	13
CONSERVATIVE	15	13
VERY CONSERVATIVE	47	9

Source: 2008 American National Election Study

legal rights to gays and lesbians. Thus, while 50 percent of nonobservant white voters supported same sex marriage and only 22 percent opposed either marriage or civil unions, only 17 percent of observant white voters favored same sex marriage and 55 percent opposed either marriage or civil unions. Likewise, 66 percent of nonobservant white voters supported adoption by same sex couples compared with only 29 percent of observant white voters.

As expected, opinions on abortion, gay marriage, and gay adoption were closely related. The correlation (Pearson's r) between opinions on gay marriage and gay adoption was .64, the correlation between opinion on abortion and opinion on gay marriage was .44, and the correlation between opinion on abortion and opinion on gay adoption was .45. Since all three questions appeared to be measuring a common underlying orientation on cultural issues, I combined them to form a scale measuring cultural liberalism versus cultural conservatism for further analysis.

There was a fairly even division within the white electorate on these cultural issues. Thirty-six percent of white voters were classified as "very liberal" or "liberal" on the cultural issues scale while 35 percent were classified as "very conservative" or "conservative." The remaining 29 percent were evenly split between those classified as "slightly liberal" and those classified as "slightly conservative." The data in Table 4.3 show that frequency of church attendance was strongly related to the location of white voters on this cultural issues scale. Among nonobservant white voters, liberals outnumbered conservatives by close to a two-to-one margin. Among observant whites, however, conservatives outnumbered liberals by a greater than three-to-one margin.

Cultural attitudes were strongly related to party identification and candidate preference among white voters, especially among those who were more politically active. Among all white voters, the correlation between the cultural issues scale and party identification was a fairly strong .43. Among those engaging in at least one activity beyond voting, though, the correlation was an even stronger .52 and among those engaging in at least two activities beyond voting the correlation was a very strong .65. As a result, the party divide on cultural issues was much greater among more politically active whites than among those who were less active. This can be seen very clearly in Figure 4.4 (see Chapter 4 color insert), which compares the cultural attitudes of white Democrats and Republicans based on their level of political activity in 2008.

About half of whites engaged in no campaign activities at all or only voted. Among that group, the party divide on cultural issues was relatively small: The distance between the average Democrat and the average Republican was only 0.5 units on the six-point cultural issues scale. And only 34 percent of these less active whites were located at the liberal or conservative end points of the scale while 36 percent were located in the two middle categories. In contrast, among the 50 percent of whites who engaged in at least one activity beyond voting, the party divide was much wider: The distance between the average Democrat and the average Republican was 2.2 units on the cultural issues scale. And 49 percent of these politically active whites were located at the liberal or conservative end points of the scale while only 21 percent were located in the two middle categories.

Opinions on cultural issues were also strongly related to presidential candidate preference among white voters in 2008. Among all white voters, 71 percent of cultural liberals (those with scores of 1 or 2 on the cultural issues scale) voted for Barack Obama compared with 39 percent of cultural moderates (those with scores of 3 or 4) and only 13 percent of cultural conservatives. And among most politically active whites, those who engaged in at least two campaign activities beyond voting, the relationship was even stronger: 82 percent of cultural liberals voted for Obama compared with 32 percent of cultural moderates and a mere 2 percent of cultural conservatives.

GROWING CONSISTENCY BETWEEN CULTURAL AND ECONOMIC ISSUES

Another important development in American politics in recent years is that opinions on cultural issues are increasingly related to opinions on the economic issues that have traditionally divided the two parties.

As recently as the 1970s and 1980s, a good many Democratic candidates and officeholders from working class constituencies combined economic liberalism with cultural conservatism. They supported government regulation of economic activity and generous spending on social programs but opposed policies such as legalized abortion and gay rights. At the same, a good many Republican candidates and officeholders from affluent and highly educated constituencies in the Northeast combined economic conservatism with cultural liberalism. They favored limits on government regulation of the economy and spending but supported abortion rights and tolerance of alternative lifestyles.

Today, few candidates or elected officials combine cultural liberalism with economic conservatism or cultural conservatism with economic liberalism. The vast majority of Republican candidates and officeholders are both cultural and economic conservatives while the vast majority of Democratic candidates and officeholders are both cultural and economic liberals. Thus, while the initial emphasis of the Tea Party movement during 2009 was on the issues of taxation and government spending, the most prominent leaders of the movement today are politicians like Michele Bachmann and Jim DeMint who combine highly conservative views on economic issues with staunch opposition to legalized abortion and same sex marriage. And consistency between cultural and economic issues has also increased among voters. For example, between 1984 and 2008, the correlation between opinions on abortion and opinions on government responsibility for health insurance among white voters increased from .07 to .28. In terms of shared variance, this means that the relationship between opinions on these two issues was sixteen times stronger in 2008 than it was in 1984.

In order to compare the consistency of opinions within and between different issue domains, I created a scale measuring liberalism on economic issues. I used four questions from the 2008 ANES to create this economic issues scale—support for government aid to blacks, government versus personal responsibility for jobs and living standards, government versus private responsibility for health insurance, and preferred level of government services and spending versus taxes. For white voters, the average correlation among these four questions was a solid .45, with a range from .29 to .55, indicating that all of these questions were measuring opinions about the role of government in the economy.

Among all white voters in 2008, the correlation between the cultural and economic issues scales was a fairly strong .44, indicating that there was a fairly high degree of consistency between cultural attitudes and economic attitudes. However, political engagement affected consistency of opinions within issue domains and between issue domains. The data displayed in Table 4.4 show that whites who were more politically active had much more consistent opinions than those who were less active. Among those who did nothing or who just voted, the average correlation within the cultural issue domain was .37, the average correlation within the economic issue domain was .33, and the average correlation between issues in the two domains was .08. So while opinions within each domain were moderately consistent, opinions on issues in the cultural and economic domains were almost unrelated. Among this group, the correlation between the cultural and economic issues scales was only .18.

In sharp contrast, among politically active whites, those who engaged in two or more activities beyond voting, there was much greater consistency both within and between domains. The average correlation within the cultural issue domain was .65, the average correlation within the economic issue domain was .61, and the average correlation between

TABLE 4.4
Average Consistency across Issue Positions for Whites in 2008 by Campaign Involvement

ISSUES	VERY LOW TO LOW	MODERATE	HIGH
CULTURAL	.37	.56	.65
ECONOMIC	.33	.40	.61
CULTURAL WITH ECONOMIC	.08	.20	.52
CULTURAL ISSUES SCALE WITH ECONOMIC ISSUES SCALE	.18	.32	.79

Source: 2008 American National Election Study

issues in the two domains was .52. Even more impressively, the correlation between cultural and economic issues scales was a very strong .79.

For politically active whites, it appears that there was almost no separation between cultural and economic issues in 2008. Opinions on cultural issues were very closely related to opinions on economic issues. For example, among politically active whites who preferred more government services and spending to lower taxes, 76 percent were pro-choice on abortion and 57 percent supported gay marriage. On the other side, among those who preferred lower taxes to more government services and spending, 68 percent were pro-life on abortion and only 11 percent supported gay marriage.

Among politically active whites, just as among elected officials and candidates, cultural attitudes and economic attitudes are closely connected. Cultural liberals are also economic liberals and cultural conservatives are also economic conservatives. As a result, not only do opinions on these two types of issues increasingly reinforce one another, but economic issues are frequently viewed in religious or moral terms. For many liberals, social welfare programs are seen as promoting a more just and equitable society while for many conservatives they are seen as undermining personal virtue and promoting dependence on a secular state.

CULTURAL ISSUES, ECONOMIC ISSUES, AND PARTY IDENTIFICATION

Cultural issues are now one of the foundations of support for political parties in the United States. However, the influence of cultural issues varies considerably based on race and political engagement. Table 4.5 compares the strength of the relationship between economic and cultural issues and party identification among various groups of voters in 2008. In general, we would expect to find the effect of cultural issues to be stronger among whites than among nonwhites, and we would expect the effect among whites to be stronger among those who are politically active than among those who are inactive.

The results displayed in Table 4.5 generally confirm our expectations. For African-Americans and Latinos, cultural issues appeared to play little

TABLE 4.5
Correlation of Party Identification with Economic and Cultural Issues
Scales by Race and Campaign Involvement in 2008

GROUP	ECONOMIC ISSUES SCALE	CULTURAL ISSUES SCALE
BLACKS	.14	.04
LATINOS	.36	.02
WHITES	.59	.36
VERY LOW INVOLVEMENT	.21	.00
LOW INVOLVEMENT	.39	.19
MODERATE INVOLVEMENT	.60	.41
HIGH INVOLVEMENT	.77	.65

Source: 2008 American National Election Study
Note: The entries shown are Pearson's r.

or no role in shaping partisan orientations in 2008. Among Latinos, only economic issues were related to party identification. Latinos with conservative views on economic issues identified themselves somewhat less with the Democratic Party than those with liberal views on economic issues, but Latinos with conservative views on cultural issues identified themselves just as much with the Democratic Party as did those with liberal views on cultural issues. African-Americans overwhelmingly identified themselves with the Democratic Party, but neither economic issues nor cultural issues seemed to explain their attachment to the party. The relatively small group of blacks with conservative views on economic issues identified itself only slightly less with the Democratic Party compared with the much larger group of blacks with liberal views on economic issues. And blacks with conservative views on cultural issues identified themselves just as much with the Democratic Party as did blacks with liberal views on cultural issues.

The evidence in Table 4.5 shows that among whites both economic and cultural issues were related to party identification, though the impact of economic issues was somewhat stronger. And both types of issues had much stronger effects among politically active whites than among politically inactive whites. In fact, among the most politically active whites, opinions on economic and cultural issues were so closely related that it is difficult to disentangle their effects on party identification. Politically active Democrats were very liberal on both economic and cultural issues while politically active Republicans were very conservative on both economic and cultural issues.

Chapter Summary

Since the 1970s, a deep cultural divide has developed within the white electorate in the United States. Among white voters today, religious beliefs and practices are stronger predictors of party affiliation and candidate preference than characteristics traditionally associated with partisan orientations such as social class and union membership. The reason for this growing cultural divide is the emergence of a new set of issues dividing Democrats and Republicans that tap into voters' moral values and religious beliefs, issues such as abortion and gay marriage. And increasingly, opinions on these cultural issues are related to opinions on more traditional economic issues, especially among the politically active. The result is that opinions on cultural issues reinforce opinions on economic issues, infusing those issues with moral overtones. Leaders of the opposing party are no longer viewed simply as mistaken in their views but as immoral. We will see in Chapter 5 that the growing cultural divide within the American electorate has also been an important factor contributing to a growing geographic divide in American politics.

CHAPTER 5

The Geographic Divide

The pundits like to slice-and-dice our country into red states and blue states; red states for Republicans, blue states for Democrats. But I've got news for them, too. We worship an awesome God in the blue states, and we don't like federal agents poking around in our libraries in the red states. We coach Little League in the blue states and yes, we've got some gay friends in the red states.... We are one people, all of us pledging allegiance to the stars and stripes, all of us defending the United States of America.

—Barack Obama, keynote address to the 2004
Democratic National Convention

Americans are closely divided, but not deeply divided.
—Morris P. Fiorina[1]

Ever since 2000, when television networks began to display the results of presidential elections with maps showing Republican states in red and Democratic states in blue, Americans have become accustomed to thinking of the United States as divided into two opposing camps—the red states versus the blue states. But according to Barack Obama, the differences between Americans who live in the red states and those who live in the blue states have been blown way out of proportion by political commentators. And Morris Fiorina agrees. In his book *Culture War*, Fiorina and his coauthors argue that while recent elections have been closely

---

[1]Morris P. Fiorina, "Beyond Red and Blue," *Stanford Magazine* (September/October, 2006): http://www.stanfordalumni.org/news/magazine/2006/sepoct/features/redvsblue.html.

contested, voters in the red states and blue states don't actually differ very much when it comes to values, lifestyles, and policy preferences.[2]

Obama's keynote address, and especially his comments on the similarities between Americans in the red states and blue states, received an enormous amount of media coverage during and after the 2004 Democratic Convention. In fact, Obama's keynote address was probably more widely discussed than John Kerry's acceptance speech. And despite his criticism of pundits for exaggerating the divisions in the country, the reaction to the speech was overwhelmingly positive. Almost overnight, Barack Obama was transformed from an obscure state legislator and U.S. senate candidate into a national political figure, setting the stage for his successful campaign for the presidency in 2008.[3]

Barack Obama was widely praised in 2004 for trying to move the nation past the bitter divisions of the Bush years. Yet Obama's own election in 2008 produced the deepest divisions between red states and blue states in recent history. The data in Table 5.1 show that there were fewer closely contested states and more landslide states in 2008 than in any other nationally competitive presidential election in the past half century, including the 2000 and 2004 elections. Only six states were decided by a margin of less than 5 percentage points while twenty-six states plus the District of Columbia were decided by a margin of at least 15 percentage points. In contrast, in 1960, twenty states were decided by a margin of less than 5 percentage points and only nine were decided by a margin of at least 15 percentage points, and in 1976, twenty states were decided by a margin of less than 5 percentage points and only eleven states plus the District of Columbia were decided by a margin of at least 15 percentage points. Moreover, the decline in the number of closely contested states and increase in the number of landslide states represented a continuation of a long-term trend. There were far fewer closely contested states and far

[2]Morris P. Fiorina with Samuel J. Abrams and Jeremy C. Pope, *Culture War? The Myth of a Polarized America*, 3rd ed. (New York: Longman, 2011), chapter 3.

[3]See John Heilemann and Mark Halperin, *Game Change: Obama and the Clintons, McCain and Palin, and the Race of a Lifetime* (New York: Harper, 2010).

TABLE 5.1

Distributions of States and Voters by State Competitiveness in Presidential Elections

	1960 (%)	1976 (%)	2000 (%)	2004 (%)	2008 (%)
STATES					
HIGH	20	20	12	11	6
MODERATE	14	11	10	10	9
LOW	7	9	6	8	9
VERY LOW	9	11	23	22	27
VOTERS					
HIGH	52	59	28	24	19
MODERATE	30	20	22	29	13
LOW	8	11	22	16	19
VERY LOW	11	10	34	31	49

Source: www.uselectionatlas.org
Note: High, 0–4.99%; Moderate, 5–9.99%; Low, 10–14.99%; Very low, 15% plus. District of Columbia included in 1976–2008 results.

more landslide states in both 2000 and 2004 than in 1960 or 1976. But the 2008 results set a new standard for geographic polarization in the modern era.

Not only have there been fewer closely contested states and more landslide states in recent presidential elections than in earlier nationally competitive elections, but several of the most populous states with the largest blocs of electoral votes have been decided by landslide margins in recent years. In earlier nationally competitive elections, almost all of the populous states were presidential battlegrounds. In 1960, for example, seven of the eight most populous states were decided by a margin of less than 5 percentage points and the only exception, New York, was decided by just over 5 percentage points. And in 1976, all eight of the most populous states were battlegrounds: California, New York, Texas, Florida, Illinois, Ohio, Pennsylvania, and Michigan were all decided by less than 5 percentage points. In contrast, in 2000 and 2004, only Florida, Ohio, and Pennsylvania were decided by less than 5 percentage points, and in 2008 only Florida and Ohio were decided by less than 5 percentage points.

As a result, the percentage of the nation's voters in battleground states has declined from 52 percent in 1960 and 59 percent in 1976 to 28 percent in 2000, 24 percent in 2004, and only 19 percent in 2008. At the same time, the percentage of voters in landslide states has grown from only 11 percent in 1960 and 10 percent in 1976 to 34 percent in 2000, 31 percent in 2004, and a remarkable 49 percent in 2008. Almost half of the nation's voters in 2008 resided in states where the presidential election was decided by a landslide margin.

While Barack Obama's seven-point margin in the national popular vote in 2008 would not be considered a landslide, the Democratic ticket carried many individual states by landslide or near-landslide margins, including several of the most populous states. For example, Obama carried California by twenty-four points, New York by twenty-five points, Illinois by twenty-five points, and Michigan by sixteen points. Of the twenty-nine states carried by the Democratic ticket, the margin was greater than ten points in twenty-two states and less than five points in only four states. However, despite the decisive Democratic victory, many individual states that voted for the Republican ticket also did so by landslide or near-landslide margins. Of the twenty-one states carried by John McCain, the GOP margin was greater than ten points in fifteen states and less than five points in only two states. And while the nation as a whole was moving in a Democratic direction between 2004 and 2008, Republicans managed to increase their margin of victory in four states: Oklahoma, Arkansas, Louisiana, and Tennessee.

A similar pattern is evident in the election results at the county level. According to an analysis by the *New York Times*, between 2004 and 2008 the Democratic share of the vote increased in 2,437 of the nation's 3,141 counties; at the same time, however, the Republican share of the vote increased in 678 counties. The Democratic share of the vote increased by more than ten points in 1,173 counties; however, the Republican share of the vote increased by more than ten points in 225 counties. Counties with the largest increases in the Democratic share of the vote were generally found in large metropolitan areas with relatively high levels of education and large concentrations of Hispanic and African-American voters. Counties with the largest increases in the Republican share of the vote were generally found in small towns and rural areas with relatively low levels of education, small minority populations, and high concentrations of southern Baptists. Many of these Republican-tilting counties are located in the Appalachian region.[4]

Contrary to the statement by Fiorina and his coauthors downplaying the significance of the red-blue divide in American politics, an examination of the 2008 electoral map reveals a country that had moved decisively in a Democratic direction since 2004 but that was more deeply divided than at any time in recent history. Although there were more blue states and fewer red states, the divide between the two was even deeper than in 2004. Across all fifty states, the average margin of victory for the winning presidential candidate increased from 13.9 points in 2004 to 16.2 points in 2008: The average margin of victory for Barack Obama was 16.8 points while the average margin of victory for John McCain was 15.4 points. In contrast, the average margin of victory for the winning presidential candidate was only 8.2 points in 1960 and only 8.9 points in 1976.

Explaining the Red-Blue Divide

The deepening divide in presidential voting between red states and blue states is itself a reflection of important differences between the social characteristics and political beliefs of voters in these two types of states. Some of these differences in social characteristics are displayed in Table 5.2, which is based on data from the 2008 American National Election Study (ANES). In this table, blue states were carried by Barack Obama by at least 5 percentage points while red states were carried by John McCain by at least 5 percentage points. The twenty-four blue states included 45 percent of voters in the 2008 ANES while the twenty red states included 35 percent of voters in the 2008 ANES.

---

[4]The county-level results can be viewed as part of an interactive map on the *New York Times* Web site: http://elections.nytimes.com/2008/results/president/map.html.

TABLE 5.2

Characteristics of Voters in Red States and Blue States in 2008

	RED STATES (%)	BLUE STATES (%)
ATTEND CHURCH		
WEEKLY	48	28
MONTHLY	12	11
OCCASIONALLY, NEVER	40	60
BORN AGAIN, EVANGELICAL	60	38
GUN OWNER	49	32
UNION HOUSEHOLD	6	18

Source: 2008 American National Election Study

Perhaps the most politically significant differences between the social characteristics of voters in the red states and voters in the blue states involved their religious orientations. Americans in the blue states may "worship an awesome God," as Barack Obama stated in his 2004 keynote address, but they appear to worship that God less frequently and less fervently than Americans in the red states. According to the data from the 2008 ANES, voters in the red states were much more likely than voters in the blue states to describe themselves as born-again or evangelical Christians and much more likely to report attending religious services every week. And these differences are even larger when we compare white voters in the red states and blue states. For example, 61 percent of white voters in the red states described themselves as born-again or evangelical Christians compared with only 33 percent of white voters in the blue states. Given the strong relationship between religious beliefs and partisanship among white voters, these differences go a long way toward explaining the red-blue divide in partisanship and presidential candidate preference. According to the ANES data, only 23 percent of whites who described themselves as born-again or evangelical Christians voted for Barack Obama while 51 percent of other whites voted for Obama.

Religion wasn't the only difference between voters in the red states and blue states. The results in Table 5.2 show that voters in the red states were somewhat less likely to be members of union households and much more likely to be gun owners than voters in the blue states. Both of these characteristics, and especially gun ownership, were associated with presidential candidate preference among white voters in 2008. According to the 2008 ANES, only 43 percent of whites in non-union households voted for Barack Obama compared with 51 percent of whites in union households, and only 33 percent of white gun owners voted for Obama compared with 53 percent of whites who were not gun owners.

As the data in Table 5.3 demonstrate, the political attitudes and behavior of voters in red states and blue states also differed fairly dramatically. According to the 2008 ANES, 67 percent of voters in the blue states cast their ballot for Barack Obama compared with only 41 percent

TABLE 5.3
Political Attitudes of Voters in Red States and Blue States in 2008

	RED STATES (%)	BLUE STATES (%)
DEMOCRAT	42	59
INDEPENDENT	7	8
REPUBLICAN	51	33
LIBERAL	22	39
MODERATE	26	26
CONSERVATIVE	52	35
PRO-CHOICE	31	53
MIXED	20	20
PRO-LIFE	49	27
FAVOR GAY MARRIAGE	29	47
CIVIL UNIONS ONLY	28	29
NEITHER	44	24
FAVOR SINGLE PAYER	38	53
NEUTRAL	10	9
OPPOSE SINGLE PAYER	51	38

Source: 2008 American National Election Study

of voters in the red states. And the difference between white voters in the blue states and red states was even more dramatic. According to the 2008 ANES, only 25 percent of white voters in the red states supported Obama compared with 58 percent of white voters in the blue states. Given the overwhelming support of nonwhite voters for Barack Obama, the fact that an outright majority of whites in the blue states voted for the Democratic candidate guaranteed that he would easily carry most of these states.

The data in Table 5.3 show that the candidate preferences of voters in the red and blue states were consistent with their underlying partisan and ideological orientations as well as their views on major campaign issues. Voters in the blue states were much less likely than their counterparts in the red states to identify with the Republican Party or to describe themselves as conservatives. They were also much more likely to describe themselves as pro-choice on abortion, to support same-sex marriage, and to favor the creation of a single-payer health care system.

Again, the differences between white voters in the red states and blue states were generally even larger than the differences for all voters reported in Table 5.3. For example, only 40 percent of white voters in the blue states identified with the Republican Party compared with 63 percent of white voters in the red states, only 38 percent of white voters in the blue states described themselves as conservative compared with 57 percent of white voters in the red states, and only 27 percent of white voters in the red states were pro-choice on abortion compared with 55 percent of white voters in the blue states.

THE RED-BLUE DIVIDE AND PRESIDENTIAL ELECTIONS

The results in the previous section demonstrate that the growing divide between red states and blue states over the past several decades has been a direct result of the ideological realignment of the American party system and the American electorate. Relatively conservative states like Texas and Georgia have been trending Republican during these years while relatively liberal states like California and New York have been trending

Democratic.[5] Texas, which was a swing state in both 1960 and 1976, has turned solidly red, having supported every Republican presidential candidate since 1980. Georgia, which was a solidly blue state in both 1960 and 1976, has also turned solidly red, having supported every Republican presidential candidate since 1992. Meanwhile, California and New York, which were swing states in 1960 and 1976, have both turned solidly blue—California has supported every Democratic presidential candidate since 1992 and New York has supported every Democratic presidential candidate since 1988.

The trend of an increasing number of states awarding an increasing number of electoral votes by landslide or near-landslide margins has had important consequences for presidential campaigns and elections in the United States. There has been a very high degree of stability in the results of recent presidential elections. The three elections between 2000 and 2008 have all been very to moderately competitive at the national level—in fact there has not been a true presidential landslide since Ronald Reagan's easy reelection victory in 1984. And there has also been a very high degree of consistency in the level of support for the two major parties across all fifty states and the District of Columbia. The correlation between the Democratic share of the vote in 2000 and the Democratic share of the vote in 2004 was .97, the highest correlation between any pair of consecutive elections since World War II. And even without George W. Bush on the ballot, the correlation between the Democratic share of the vote in 2004 and the Democratic share of the vote in 2008 was only slightly lower, at .95. With few exceptions, the same states were strongly Democratic in all three elections and the same states were strongly Republican in all three elections.

Before the campaign even begins, candidates of both major parties are virtually assured of winning a large bloc of states that their party has won by a comfortable margin in every recent presidential election. Democratic candidates have carried thirteen states plus the District of Columbia with 179 electoral votes by a margin of at least 5 percentage points in all three

---

[5]The growing regional divide in American politics is discussed in depth in Earl Black and Merle Black, *Divided America: The Ferocious Power Struggle in American Politics* (New York: Simon & Schuster, 2007).

elections between 2000 and 2008. Meanwhile, Republican candidates have carried twenty states with 167 electoral votes by a margin of at least 5 percentage points in all three elections. On Election Day 2012, it is very likely that California, Connecticut, Delaware, the District of Columbia, Hawaii, Illinois, Maine, Maryland, Massachusetts, New Jersey, New York, Rhode Island, Vermont, and Washington will again end up in the Democratic column and that Alabama, Alaska, Arizona, Arkansas, Georgia, Idaho, Kansas, Kentucky, Louisiana, Mississippi, Nebraska, North Dakota, Oklahoma, South Carolina, South Dakota, Tennessee, Texas, Utah, West Virginia, and Wyoming will again end up the Republican column.

Relatively few states are now seriously contested in presidential elections. A total of seventeen states with 192 electoral votes have not decisively favored one party or the other in all three elections between 2000 and 2008. That's more than enough to swing the outcome of a presidential election. But seven of those states appear to lean toward one party. Five states with sixty-three electoral votes—Michigan, Minnesota, Oregon, Pennsylvania, and Wisconsin—have supported the Democratic nominee in all three recent elections, although sometimes narrowly, while two states with thirteen electoral votes—Missouri and Montana—have supported the Republican nominee in all three recent elections, although sometimes narrowly. Only ten states, with 116 electoral votes, have supported presidential candidates from both parties. Those ten states—Colorado, Florida, Indiana, Iowa, Nevada, New Hampshire, New Mexico, North Carolina, Ohio, and Virginia—will most likely again be key battlegrounds in 2012.

THE GROWING RED-BLUE DIVIDE IN THE SENATE

Growing geographic polarization has had important consequences for U.S. Senate elections as well as presidential elections.[6] We can use the results of the most recent presidential election to measure the partisan orientations of states represented by Democratic and Republican sena-

[6]See Alan I. Abramowitz, "U.S. Senate Elections in a Polarized Era," in *The U.S. Senate: From Deliberation to Dysfunction,* ed. Burdett A. Loomis (Washington, DC: Congressional Quarterly Press, 2012).

TABLE 5.4

The Partisan Orientations of States Represented by Incumbent U.S. Senators

PARTISAN ORIENTATION	96TH SENATE (1979–80) (%)	112TH SENATE (2011–12) (%)
SUPPORTIVE	37	71
COMPETITIVE	40	12
OPPOSITIONAL	23	17
TOTAL	100	100

Source: Data compiled by author
Note: Supportive, percentage of states won by a margin of at least 5 percentage points by the candidate of a senator's party; Oppositional, percentage of states won by a margin of at least 5 percentage points by the candidate of the opposing party; Competitive, percentage of states won by a margin of less than 5 percentage points.

tors (see Table 5.4). Here, I have classified states won by a margin of at least 5 percentage points by the candidate of a senator's party as "supportive," classified states won by a margin of at least 5 percentage points by the candidate of the opposing party as "oppositional," and classified states won by a margin of less than 5 percentage points as "competitive."

The data displayed in Table 5.4 show that compared with the Senate of the late 1970s, the current Senate includes a much larger number of members who represent states in which their party is in a dominant position and a much smaller number of members who represent swing states and states where the opposing party is dominant. That's partly because there are so many more states now that are dominated by one party and partly because there is more partisan voting in Senate elections. As a result, it has become more difficult for a candidate from the minority party in a state to win a Senate election.

The partisan orientation of the electorate in a state has a strong influence on the outcomes of Senate elections. Between 2002 and 2010 there were 172 Senate contests. Of those 172 contests, 32, or 19 percent, produced a switch in party control. However, the probability of a switch in party control was strongly related to the strength of the party defending the seat. Of the ninety-one contests that involved

Democratic seats in blue states or Republican seats in red states, only 3 percent produced a switch in party control. In contrast, of the thirty-four contests that took place in swing states, 32 percent produced a switch in party control, and of the twenty-three contests that involved Democratic seats in red states or Republican seats in blue states, 39 percent produced a switch in party control. To put it slightly differently, even though 53 percent of all Senate contests during this period involved either a Democratic seat in a blue state or a Republican seat in a red state, only 9 percent of all switches in party control occurred in those contests.

The fact that compared with thirty or forty years ago many more senators now represent states where their party is clearly favored and many fewer represent either swing states or states where the opposing party is clearly favored has had important consequences for the way the Senate operates. There is a fairly strong relationship between senators' voting records and the strength of their party in their state. The less one can count on winning with votes from one's own party, the more one has to worry about appealing to independents and voters who normally support the opposing party. Therefore, Democrats who represent swing states or Republican-leaning states tend to have more moderate voting records than Democrats who represent strongly Democratic states, and Republicans who represent swing states or Democratic-leaning states tend to have more moderate voting records than Republicans who represent strongly Republican states.

It is no accident that the two Republican senators with the most moderate voting records in the 111th Congress were Olympia Snowe and Susan Collins, who both represented solidly blue Maine, and it is no accident that the Democratic senator with the most moderate voting record in the 111th Congress was Ben Nelson, who represented solidly red Nebraska. There are very few senators left who represent states where their party is in the minority. The growing number of Democrats from solidly blue states and Republicans from solidly red states has been an important factor contributing to the decline of moderates and the rise of ideological polarization in the Senate over the past several decades.

THE GROWING RED-BLUE DIVIDE IN THE HOUSE
OF REPRESENTATIVES

The Senate is not the only chamber of Congress that has been affected by growing geographic polarization in recent years. House districts have also become increasingly divided along party lines.[7] We can classify the partisan orientations of House districts in the same way that we classified the partisan orientations of states—based on the results of the most recent presidential election in the district. Districts in which the winning presidential candidate's vote share was at least 10 percentage points greater than his national vote share were classified as safe for that candidate's party. Districts in which the winning candidate's vote share was greater than his national vote share by only 5 percentage points or less were classified as marginal.

The presidential vote is a powerful predictor of the outcomes of House elections. For example, in 2010, Democratic candidates won all 112 House contests in safe Democratic districts while Republican candidates won 95 of the 99 House contests in safe Republican districts. Despite the strong Republican tide in 2010, Democrats did not lose a single seat in a safe Democratic district. However, they lost forty-one of their sixty-nine seats in marginal districts. Similarly, despite the strong Democratic tide in 2006, Republicans lost only two of their ninety-nine seats in safe Republican districts. However, they lost eighteen of their sixty-three seats in marginal districts.

Marginal districts account for the large majority of the seat swing in House elections. However, the data displayed in Figure 5.1 show that there are now far fewer marginal districts and far more safe districts than there were during the 1980s or 1990s. And contrary to the view of many pundits and political commentators, these data also show that partisan gerrymandering has not been responsible for the increasing number of safe districts and the decreasing number of marginal districts.

Redistricting, the process of redrawing congressional district lines that occurs after each decennial census, is often blamed for declining

---

[7]See Bruce I. Oppenheimer, "Deep Red and Blue Congressional Districts," in *Congress Reconsidered*, 8th ed., ed. Lawrence C. Dodd and Bruce I. Oppenheimer (Washington, DC: Congressional Quarterly Press, 2005).

FIGURE 5.1

Numbers of Safe and Competitive House Districts before and
after Redistricting, 1980–2010

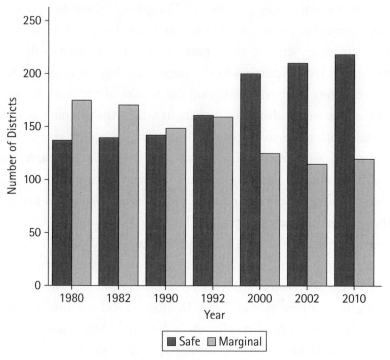

Source: Gary Jacobson and data compiled by author

competition in House elections. Partisan mapmakers, usually state legislators, using sophisticated electronic databases and computer programs, are
accused of drawing district lines to protect themselves and their congressional colleagues.[8] There is no doubt that redistricting is often a highly
partisan and contentious process. But protecting incumbents is only one
possible goal in redistricting and it is not always the dominant one. Some
redistricting plans are designed to maximize seats for one party, not to
maximize safe seats for incumbents.[9]

---

[8]See for example Mark Monmonier, *Bushmanders and Bullwinkles: How Politicians Manipulate
Electronic Maps and Census Data to Win Elections* (Chicago: University of Chicago Press, 2001).

[9]For a balanced assessment of the consequences of redistricting for competition in congressional
elections, see Thomas E. Mann and Bruce E. Cain, eds., *Party Lines: Competition, Partisanship and
Congressional Redistricting* (Washington, DC: Brookings Institution Press, 2005).

In fact, it appears that gerrymandering has been a relatively minor factor in the growing ratio of safe districts to marginal districts in recent years.[10] Between 1980 and 2010, the number of safe House districts increased from 133 to 213 while the number of marginal districts decreased from 170 to 112. However, very little of this change can be attributed to redistricting. Between 1980 and 2010, there were three redistricting cycles—in 1981–82, 1991–92, and 2001–02. Following the first one, in 1982, the number of safe districts rose from 133 to 137 while the number of marginal districts fell from 170 to 166, not much of a change. Ten years later, following the 1991–92 redistricting cycle, the number of safe districts rose from 138 to 157 but the number of marginal districts also rose, from 147 to 156. Finally, after the most recent redistricting cycle in 2001–02, the number of safe districts increased from 200 to 205 while the number of marginal districts fell from 122 to 110—again not a very large change. It remains to be seen what effect the 2011–12 round of redistricting has on district competitiveness but, based on the results of the last three rounds, we would not expect any dramatic change in the numbers of safe and marginal districts.

The data in Figure 5.1 show that the large majority of the change in the numbers of safe and marginal House districts since 1980 occurred between redistricting cycles, especially between 1992 and 2000. During that decade, even though no district lines were redrawn, the number of safe districts increased from 157 to 200 while the number of marginal districts decreased from 156 to 122.

So if partisan gerrymandering is not responsible for the increasing red-blue divide in the House of Representatives, what is? The answer appears to be a combination of ideological realignment within the electorate, a growing number of heavily African-American and Latino districts, and migration patterns that have increased the political homogeneity of many cities, counties, and neighborhoods in the United States.

Just as with states, House districts have been trending Democratic or Republican depending on their ideological tendencies. Relatively

---

[10]Alan I. Abramowitz, Brad Alexander, and Matthew Gunning, "Incumbency, Redistricting and the Decline of Competition in U.S. House Elections," *Journal of Politics* 68 (2006): 75–88.

conservative districts, including many in the southern states, have been trending Republican. In the 1970s, a large majority of House districts in the Deep South were still sending conservative Democrats to Congress. Today, except for majority-minority districts, almost all of those districts are represented by conservative Republicans. At the same time, relatively liberal districts, including many in the metropolitan areas of the Midwest, Northeast, and Pacific Coast, have been trending Democratic. In the 1970s, many House districts in the New York, Chicago, and San Francisco suburbs were sending moderate Republicans to Congress. Today, a large majority of those districts are represented by liberal Democrats.

As a result of the growing proportions of African-Americans, Latinos, and other nonwhites in the U.S. population and the application of the federal Voting Rights Act, there has been a substantial increase in the number of majority-minority districts in the House since the 1980s. The number of majority-minority districts has grown from twenty-three in 1980 to seventy-seven in 2010, and the number is certain to increase further following the 2011–12 round of redistricting as a result of the increase in the nonwhite share of the population between 2000 and 2010. These majority-minority districts tend to be strongly Democratic, often giving over 80 percent of their votes to the party's presidential and congressional candidates. Of the seventy-seven majority-minority House districts in the 112th Congress, all but three are safe Democratic districts and all but two were represented by Democrats. In fact, more than two-thirds of the 106 safe Democratic districts in the 112th House are majority-minority districts.

Finally, migration patterns within the United States have been contributing to growing geographic polarization, as Americans increasingly choose to live in communities made up of residents with similar backgrounds, values, and lifestyles.[11] These choices are not necessarily based on politics. It's not that Democrats are choosing to live among other Democrats and Republicans are choosing to live among other Republicans. It's that Americans are choosing to live in communities

---

[11]Bill Bishop with Robert G. Cushing, *The Big Sort: Why the Clustering of Like-Minded Americans Is Tearing Us Apart* (Boston: Houghton Mifflin, 2008).

where the residents have similar backgrounds, values, and lifestyles to themselves and those backgrounds, values, and lifestyles are strongly related to political outlook.

Race and ethnicity are the most obvious influence on these residential decisions—decades after the end of laws requiring racial segregation in housing, most Americans still prefer to live in neighborhoods where their own racial or ethnic group is in the majority. But other factors also contribute to political segregation, especially lifestyle preferences. Thus, married couples with children tend to gravitate toward suburban neighborhoods with large homes and good public schools; religious individuals and families generally choose to live close to their preferred house of worship; and gays, lesbians, and young singles tend to gravitate toward inner city neighborhoods that meet their cultural and lifestyle needs.

The end result of these residential choices is increasing geographic polarization. As Bill Bishop has pointed out in his book, *The Big Sort*, Americans living in "landslide counties," those that voted Democratic or Republican for president by a margin of at least 20 percentage points, increased from 28 percent of the population in 1976 to 45 percent in 2000 and then to 48 percent in 2008.[12] That increase in geographic polarization has affected the partisan composition of districts represented by elected officials at all levels of government. More and more city council districts, state legislative districts, and U.S. House districts are now dominated by one party and that development has had important consequences for elections, representation, and governance.

One-party domination means that general elections no longer choose elected officials in many cases. In strongly Democratic and Republican districts, the most important choices are made in party primaries, which tend to be dominated by strong partisans with relatively extreme ideological views. As a result, Democrats chosen in safe Democratic districts tend to be very liberal while Republicans chosen in safe Republican districts tend to be very conservative. There is little incentive for these elected officials to seek compromises with the opposing party because such compromises

---

[12]Bill Bishop with Robert G. Cushing, *The Big Sort*.

could upset their own party's supporters and potentially lead to a primary challenge. These and other consequences of growing geographic polarization will be discussed in greater detail in Chapter 7.

CHAPTER SUMMARY

When it comes to political geography, Americans today are not only closely divided; they are also deeply divided. Whether one focuses on states, House districts, counties, or just about any other geographic unit, it is clear that by any reasonable standard the partisan divide is much deeper today than it was thirty or forty years ago. There are far more solidly red and solidly blue states, congressional districts, and counties than there were in the past and far fewer closely divided states, congressional districts, and counties. Moreover, these differences in party affiliation and voting behavior reflect differences in fundamental beliefs about religion, morality, and the role of government in American society.

The result of this growing red-blue divide is that general elections have become less competitive, primary elections have become more important in choosing elected officials, and incentives for bipartisan cooperation and compromise have been eroded. And because this trend is not a result of partisan gerrymandering but of important changes in American politics and society, it is unlikely to be reversed any time soon.

CHAPTER 6

The Polarized Public and the Rise of the Tea Party Movement

People are already saying now you need to weave and dodge, now you need to switch, now you need to give up your conservative message. You need to become a moderate. You need to give up the Tea Party.... The Tea Party message is not a radical message. It's not an extreme message. What is extreme is a $2 trillion deficit.

—Rand Paul, Republican Senate candidate in Kentucky, primary election victory speech, May 18, 2010

The Republican Party would be really smart to start trying to absorb as much of the Tea Party movement as possible.

—Sarah Palin, keynote speech to the National Tea Party Convention, February 6, 2010

The rise of the Tea Party movement during 2009 and 2010 was a direct result of the growing polarization of the American electorate and, specifically, the growing conservatism of the electoral base of the Republican Party. But the Tea Party movement was not just a reflection of growing polarization. By helping to move the Republican Party even further to the right since 2008, the Tea Party movement has contributed significantly to that polarization.

In the 2010 Senate elections, Tea Party supporters helped conservative insurgents, including Sharron Angle in Nevada, Christine O'Donnell in Delaware, and Rand Paul in Kentucky to upset more moderate establishment–backed candidates in Republican primaries. In the House of Representatives, the large cadre of Tea Party–supported freshmen elected in 2010 helped to produce the most conservative and most polarized House in modern times. And in 2011, Tea Party supporters exerted a strong influence on the early stages of the 2012 Republican presidential nomination race—providing encouragement and support for conservative candidates, including Minnesota Congresswoman Michele Bachmann and Texas Governor Rick Perry.

The Tea Party movement has attracted enormous attention from journalists, candidates, and elected officials since it first appeared on the U.S. political scene in early 2009. However, there has been considerable disagreement among political observers about the size of the movement; the motivations of those participating in Tea Party protests; the role played by wealthy individuals, conservative groups, and media figures in fomenting these protests; and the potential long-term impact of the movement.[1] A key question raised by the spread of Tea Party protests and the emergence of Tea Party candidates in numerous House, Senate, and gubernatorial elections in 2010 is whether this movement represents a new force in American politics or whether it is simply the latest, and perhaps the noisiest, manifestation of the long-term rightward shift of the Republican Party—a shift that can be seen as part of a larger trend toward increasing partisan polarization in American politics.[2]

Political analysts aligned with the liberal wing of the Democratic Party have tended to criticize the Tea Party movement as a largely top-down phenomenon driven by well-funded, conservative interest groups and media figures.[3] It is clear that organizations such as Americans for Prosperity and Freedom Works have provided important logistical support for the movement and that conservative media figures, mainly associated

---

[1]See, for example, Jacob Weisberg, "A Tea Party Taxonomy," *Newsweek* (September 27, 2010): 32.
[2]For a scholarly perspective on the emergence of the Tea Party movement and its impact on the Republican Party, see Vanessa Williamson, Theda Skocpol, and John Coggin, "The Tea Party and the Remaking of Republican Conservatism," *Perspectives on Politics* 9 (2011): 25–44.
[3]See, for example, Paul Waldman, "Tea Party Standard," *The American Prospect* (September 21, 2010): http://www.prospect.org/cs/articles?article=tea_party_standard.

with Fox News, have played crucial roles in publicizing and encouraging attendance at Tea Party rallies.[4] However, these efforts could not have succeeded without the existence of a large, receptive audience among the public. Any successful social movement requires both leadership and organization and a grassroots army of sympathizers to respond to those leaders and organizations, and the Tea Party movement is no exception.

This chapter will examine the sources of support for the Tea Party movement within the American public in order to explain why the Tea Party movement emerged when it did, immediately following the election of a Democratic president and Congress in 2008, and whether the movement is likely to remain a significant force in American politics in 2012 and beyond. Using data from American National Election Study (ANES) surveys over the past several decades, I argue that grassroots support for the Tea Party movement can best be understood as a product of the increasing conservatism of the Republican Party's electoral base over the past several decades. While only a small fraction of all Republican voters actually participated in Tea Party protests, the increasing conservatism and activism of the GOP base has produced a large cadre of politically engaged sympathizers from which such participants can be recruited.

Along with a growing number of conservative Republican activists, the other factor crucial to the emergence of the Tea Party movement at the grass roots was the Democratic victory in the 2008 election, and especially the election of Barack Obama as president. Obama's mixed racial heritage, his ambitious policy agenda, and the extraordinarily diverse coalition of liberals, young people, and racial minorities who supported him in 2008 all contributed to a powerful negative reaction on the part of many economic and social conservatives aligned with the Republican Party and among some whites who were simply upset about having a black man in the White House.

The intense negative reaction to Obama among many Republican voters as well as Republican leaders can be seen as a reflection of the growing racial divide between the parties as well as the growing ideological

---

[4]Paul Bedard, "Poll: Tea Party Amped Up by Fox, Glenn Beck," *USNEWS.com* (July 19): http://politics.usnews.com'/news/washington-whispers/aricles/2010/01/19/poll-tea-party-amped-up-by-fox-glenn-beck.html.

divide between the parties. While any Democratic president pursuing a liberal policy agenda would probably have provoked a strong reaction from conservatives, Obama's presence in the White House may have intensified that reaction by activating racial fears and resentments among some whites. These fears and resentments were of course stoked by right-wing politicians, media commentators, and Web sites.

A recurring theme on the right since even before the 2008 election has been that because of his mixed racial heritage, Barack Obama's values were different from those of the large majority of white Americans. The widespread promotion by right-wing talk show hosts and Web sites of claims that Obama was really a Muslim and may not have been born in the United States sought to exploit this sentiment.[5] Acceptance of these beliefs, along with intense opposition to specific policies, such as the economic stimulus and health care reform, helped to create a large pool of individuals who were receptive to calls for action by conservative organizations and media figures during 2009–10.

BREWING THE TEA: THE GROWTH OF THE CONSERVATIVE REPUBLICAN BASE, 1972–2008

In order to understand the origins of the Tea Party movement, one needs to go back many years before the appearance of Barack Obama on the national political scene. The Tea Party movement can best be understood in the context of the long-term growth of partisan-ideological polarization within the American electorate and especially the growing conservatism of the Republican Party's electoral base.

Over the past several decades, the U.S. party system has undergone an ideological realignment at both the elite and mass levels. At the elite level, conservative Democrats and liberal Republicans who once held key leadership positions in the congressional parties have almost disappeared, and the number of moderates in both parties has gradually diminished, leaving a

---

[5]Sheryl G. Stolberg, "In Defining Obama, Misperceptions Stick," *New York Times* (August 18, 2010): A-19.

predominantly liberal Democratic Party battling a predominantly conservative Republican Party.[6] At the mass level, as the evidence data in Chapter 3 demonstrated, change has not been quite as dramatic but citizens have gradually brought their party loyalties into line with their ideological orientations, with the result that Democratic identifiers have been moving to the left while Republican identifiers have been moving to the right.[7]

While the alignment of partisanship with ideology is not as close at the mass level as it is at the elite level, we have seen that within the American public the sharpest ideological divide is found among the most politically engaged citizens. In general, partisan-ideological polarization is greatest among the most interested, informed, and active members of the public: active Democrats are far more liberal than inactive Democrats and active Republicans are far more conservative than inactive Republicans. Moreover, as the parties have become more polarized, the size of each party's activist base has been increasing.[8]

Rather than turning off the public, the growing polarization of the parties appears to have led to increased interest and participation in the electoral process since the 1980s, which could be explained by the fact that citizens generally perceive that more is at stake in elections. Table 6.1 displays the trend in electoral participation among Republican identifiers over the past six decades, according to data from the ANES. The electoral participation scale is based on responses to six questions about election-related activities—voting; trying to influence someone else's vote; displaying a campaign button, yard sign, or bumper sticker; giving money to a

---

[6]On the rise of polarization in Congress, see Keith T. Poole and Howard Rosenthal, *Congress: A Political-Economic History of Roll Call Voting* (New York: Oxford University Press, 2000). See also Barbara Sinclair, "The New World of U.S. Senators," in *Congress Reconsidered*, 8th ed., ed. Lawrence C. Dodd and Bruce I. Oppenheimer (Washington, DC: Congressional Quarterly Press, 2005); and Lawrence C. Dodd and Bruce I. Oppenheimer, "A Decade of Republican Control: The House of Representatives, 1995–2005," in *Congress Reconsidered*, 8th ed., ed. Dodd and Oppenheimer (Washington, DC: Congressional Quarterly Press, 2005). On polarization in the 112th Congress, see Alan I. Abramowitz, "Expect Confrontation, Not Compromise," *PS: Political Science and Politics* 44 (2011): 293–95.

[7]Alan I. Abramowitz, *The Disappearing Center: Engaged Citizens, Polarization and American Democracy* (New Haven: Yale University Press, 2010); see also, Joseph Bafumi and Robert Y. Shapiro, "A New Partisan Voter," *Journal of Politics* 71 (2009): 1–24.

[8]Abramowitz, *The Disappearing Center*, chapter 2.

TABLE 6.1

Campaign Activism by Decade among Republican Identifiers

CAMPAIGN ACTIVITIES	52–60 (%)	62–70 (%)	72–80 (%)	82–90 (%)	92–00 (%)	02–08 (%)
0	13	16	21	28	22	13
1	41	42	39	40	39	37
2	24	22	23	21	26	31
3+	22	20	17	11	13	19

Source: American National Election Studies Cumulative File (1952–2008)
Note: Scores indicate the number of election activities a respondent reported engaging in (see text).

candidate or party; attending a campaign rally; and working for a campaign. Therefore, scores range from 0 for individuals who engaged in no activities to 6 for those who engaged in all six activities.

The data in Table 6.1 show that the percentage of Republican identifiers participating in two or more activities—generally individuals who did more than just vote—reached a low point during the 1980s but then rebounded in the 1990s and reached an all-time high in the most recent decade. As partisan polarization has increased in recent years, so has the level of activism of Republican identifiers. While only about a third of Republican identifiers reported engaging in at least two activities in the 1980s, fully half reported engaging in at least two activities in the 2000s. At the same time, the percentage of Republican identifiers engaging in at least three activities almost doubled, going from 11 percent in the 1980s to 19 percent in the most recent period.

These results indicate that over the past three decades there has been a marked increase in the size of the activist base of the Republican Party—an increase that preceded the rise of the Tea Party movement. Moreover, as the GOP's activist base was growing, it was also becoming increasingly conservative. Figure 6.1 displays the trend in the average score of Republican identifiers on a seven-point liberal-conservative scale between the 1970s and the 2000s. This is as far back in time as we can go since the ANES did not begin asking this question until 1972.

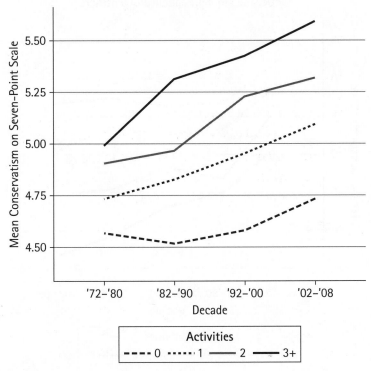

FIGURE 6.1

Average Conservatism of Republican Identifiers by Decade

Source: ANES Cumulative File, 1972–2008

The data in Figure 6.1 show that over this time period there has been a fairly steady increase in the average conservatism score of Republican identifiers. Rank-and-file Republicans have been following their party's leaders to the right. Moreover, the data show that this increase has been greatest among the most active party identifiers—those who presumably pay the most attention to what their party's leaders are doing. While the increase in conservatism was fairly modest among inactive Republicans, it was very substantial among the most active group—those engaging in at least three activities. This group was the most conservative to begin with and it became much more conservative during this time period, going from an average score of 5.0 to an average score of 5.6 on the 7-point scale.

Thus far we have seen that the most active segment of the Republican base almost doubled in size between the 1980s and 2000s and that it also

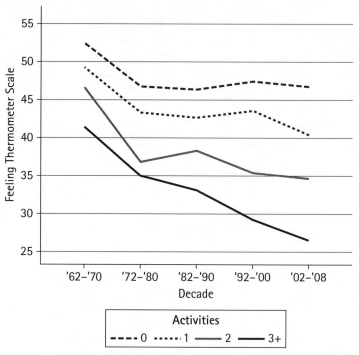

FIGURE 6.2

Average Feeling Thermometer Rating of Democratic Presidential Candidate
by Decade among Republican Identifiers

Source: ANES Cumulative File, 1962–2008

became considerably more conservative during this time period. But that was not the only important shift in outlook that occurred. Figure 6.2 displays the trend in the average rating of Democratic presidential candidates by Republican identifiers on the feeling thermometer scale over the past five decades. Since 1968, the ANES has asked respondents to rate a variety of individuals and groups on this feeling thermometer scale, which ranges from 0 (very cold) to 100 (very warm). A score of 50 is considered neutral.

The data in Figure 6.2 show that as Republican identifiers have become increasingly conservative, they have also become increasingly negative in their evaluations of Democratic presidential candidates. A very similar trend is evident in evaluations of the Democratic Party itself. And once again, the most dramatic change occurred among the most active Republican identifiers—those engaging in at least three election activities.

Among this group, the average feeling thermometer rating of Democratic presidential candidates fell from a lukewarm forty-two degrees in the late 1960s to a very chilly twenty-six degrees in the 2000s.

The data from the ANES surveys show that over the past several decades, the active Republican base has become increasingly conservative and increasingly hostile to the Democratic Party and its presidential candidates. By 2008, as the data in Table 6.2 demonstrate, the active Republican base had been primed to respond positively to calls from conservative organizations and media figures to engage in protest activity against a newly elected Democratic president and Congress with an ambitious liberal policy agenda. This table compares the social characteristics

TABLE 6.2

Social Characteristics and Political Attitudes of Active Republicans versus Overall Electorate in 2008

	ACTIVE REPUBLICANS (%)	OVERALL ELECTORATE (%)
SOCIAL CHARACTERISTICS		
WHITE	92	75
MALE	50	45
COLLEGE GRADUATES	44	29
18–29 YEARS OLD	16	21
50 AND OLDER	50	43
INCOME $75,000 OR MORE	55	37
WEEKLY CHURCHGOER	50	33
POLITICAL ATTITUDES		
CONSERVATIVE	83	42
VERY CONSERVATIVE	59	26
OPPOSE HEALTH CARE REFORM	74	37
PRO-LIFE ON ABORTION	58	42
OPPOSE GAY MARRIAGE	83	61
FAVOR REDUCED GOVERNMENT ROLE	75	41
NEGATIVE RATING OF OBAMA	69	29
POSITIVE RATING OF PALIN	84	46

Source: 2008 ANES

and political attitudes of active Republican identifiers (those who engaged in two or more election-related activities in 2008) with the social characteristics and political attitudes of the overall electorate.

The data in Table 6.2 reflect the results of four decades of growing racial, cultural, and ideological polarization. In 2008, active Republicans were overwhelmingly white, more religious, and much more conservative than the overall electorate. Compared with the electorate as a whole, active Republicans were much more likely to place themselves on the right side of the seven-point liberal-conservative scale, to oppose the creation of a single-payer health care system, to oppose gay marriage, to take a pro-life position on the issue of abortion, and to favor a reduced role for government in dealing with social problems. They were also much more likely to give Barack Obama a negative rating and Sarah Palin a positive rating on the feeling thermometer scale. Given the decidedly conservative and anti-Obama attitudes of the active Republican base, the size of this group, and its relatively high level of previous political engagement, the success of the Tea Party movement in mobilizing large numbers of anti-Obama protesters is not surprising.

DRINKING THE TEA: ANALYZING PUBLIC SUPPORT FOR THE TEA PARTY MOVEMENT IN 2010

While several million individuals may have taken part in Tea Party protests or contributed money to Tea Party organizations or candidates since the movement first appeared on the political scene in early 2009, these active participants clearly constitute only a small fraction of a much larger group of Tea Party sympathizers. I will concentrate here on analyzing the sources of support for the Tea Party movement among the American public, using data from the October 2010 wave of the ANES Evaluations of Government and Society Survey (EGSS).[9] These data show that the

---

[9]The October 2010 survey is the first of several cross-sectional studies being conducted by ANES, in 2010, 2011, and 2012, to test new instrumentation and measure public opinion between the 2008 and 2012 presidential elections. The surveys are being conducted entirely on the Internet using nationally representative probability samples. Respondents are members of the Knowledge Networks Knowledge Panel, an omnibus panel of respondents recruited using telephone and address-based sampling methods, who are provided free Internet access and equipment when necessary.

growing polarization of the American electorate and specifically the growing conservatism of the electoral base of the Republican Party paved the way for the rise of the Tea Party movement in 2009.

It is important to understand the characteristics and attitudes of Tea Party supporters within the public because it is from this group that the protest participants and contributors were recruited. It is also important to understand this larger group because it constitutes a bloc of voters that Tea Party candidates can look to for electoral support—a constituency that has proven large enough to carry a number of Tea Party candidates to victory over more mainstream or moderate candidates in Republican primaries. Tea Party supporters undoubtedly played major roles in the upset victories of Sharron Angle in Nevada, Christine O'Donnell in Delaware, and Ken Buck in Colorado in 2010 over candidates backed by the Republican establishment. However, the fact that all three of these candidates went on to lose in the general election, possibly costing the Republican Party three U.S. Senate seats, suggests that the Tea Party movement, by supporting candidates whose views are far to the right of the overall electorate, poses serious risks for the GOP in areas that are not solidly Republican.

The 2010 EGSS included questions about the Tea Party movement and a series of questions about current domestic policy issues in addition to questions about racial attitudes, political activities, and demographic characteristics. This made it possible to analyze the sources of support for the Tea Party movement and to compare the political activities, social characteristics, and the racial and political attitudes of Tea Party supporters with the attitudes of members of the general public and Republicans who did not support the Tea Party movement.

Respondents in the EGSS were asked if they considered themselves supporters of the Tea Party movement. Those who described themselves as supporters were then asked a follow-up question about whether they supported the Tea Party strongly or not too strongly. Overall, 23 percent of the survey respondents described themselves as supporters of the Tea Party movement.

Table 6.3 compares the social characteristics and political attitudes of Tea Party supporters with those of nonsupporters. The findings regarding

TABLE 6.3
Social Characteristics and Political Attitudes of Tea Party Supporters versus Nonsupporters

	TEA PARTY SUPPORTERS (%)	NONSUPPORTERS (%)
SOCIAL CHARACTERISTICS AND ATTITUDES		
AGE > 44	70	59
WHITE	85	75
MALE	63	45
MARRIED	62	49
INCOME $75,000+	31	24
COLLEGE GRAD	27	30
BORN AGAIN/EVANGELICAL	52	33
WEEKLY CHURCHGOER	50	36
BELIEVE BIBLE, ACTUAL WORD OF GOD	49	28
GUN OWNER	43	29
POLITICAL AND RACIAL ATTITUDES		
REPUBLICAN IDEOLOGY OR LEAN	86	32
CONSERVATIVE IDEOLOGY	85	29
DISLIKE OBAMA	84	27
LIKE PALIN	77	19
BIRTHER	44	22
OPPOSE ENDING "DON'T ASK, DON'T TELL"	67	31
OPPOSE CLEAN ENERGY	74	21
OPPOSE HEALTH CARE REFORM	81	33
OPPOSE STEM CELL RESEARCH	66	29
OPPOSE ECONOMIC STIMULUS	87	41
DISAGREE BLACKS ARE VICTIMS	74	39
DISAGREE BLACKS GOTTEN LESS	77	42
AGREE BLACKS NEED TO TRY HARDER	66	36
AGREE NO FAVORS FOR BLACKS	80	48

Source: ANES Evaluations of Government and Society Survey, October 2010

the social characteristics of Tea Party supporters indicate that the widely held stereotype of this group as made up predominantly of older white males is largely correct. Tea Party supporters were overwhelmingly white, they were somewhat older than nonsupporters, and they were very disproportionately male. In addition, Tea Party supporters were somewhat more affluent than nonsupporters and they were considerably more religious than nonsupporters and more likely to be gun owners. In terms of education, Tea Party supporters were slightly less likely than nonsupporters to have graduated from college. In general, Tea Party supporters reflected the characteristics of active Republicans.

However, when we turn our attention from social characteristics to political attitudes the differences between Tea Party supporters and the overall electorate become very striking. Although some Tea Party leaders have tried to stress the movement's independence from the Republican Party, it is clear from these data and from other surveys that supporters of the Tea Party movement overwhelmingly identify with the Republican Party. In this case, 86 percent of Tea Party supporters were Republican identifiers or independents leaning toward the Republican Party compared with only 32 percent of nonsupporters. Tea Party supporters make up a very large proportion of the Republican electoral base. According to the EGSS data, 45 percent of all Republican identifiers and leaners and 63 percent of strong Republican identifiers described themselves as supporters of the Tea Party movement.

Going along with the strongly Republican party loyalties of Tea Party supporters, the data from the EGSS show that compared with nonsupporters, Tea Party supporters held much more negative views of President Obama and much more positive views of the Republican politician who was perhaps most frequently associated with the Tea Party movement during 2009 and 2010—Sarah Palin. Fully 84 percent of Tea Party supporters had an unfavorable opinion of Barack Obama, and 77 percent had a favorable opinion of Sarah Palin. In contrast, only 27 percent of nonsupporters had an unfavorable opinion of Obama, and only 19 percent had a favorable opinion of Palin. And Tea Party supporters were also much more likely than nonsupporters to have doubts about whether Barack Obama was born in the United States: 44 percent of sup-porters believed that Obama either probably or definitely was not born in the United States compared with only 22 percent of nonsupporters.

When it comes to ideology and issue positions, the data in Table 6.3 show that Tea Party supporters were far to the right of the rest of the public. Eighty-five percent of Tea Party supporters described themselves as conserva-tive compared with only 29 percent of nonsupporters. Similarly, compared with the overall public, Tea Party supporters were much more likely to take the conservative side on a wide variety of policy issues, opposing key Obama Administration initiatives: repeal of the "don't ask, don't tell" policy toward gays in the military, government support for clean energy development, health care reform, stem cell research, and the economic stimulus program.

The fact that Tea Party supporters were much more likely than non-supporters to identify themselves as born again or evangelical Christians and to accept a literal interpretation of the Bible as well as the fact that they were substantially more opposed to repealing the "don't ask, don't tell" policy toward gays in the military suggest that support for the Tea Party was based on social as well as economic conservatism. Moreover, the fact that Tea Party supporters scored substantially higher than nonsupporters on four questions measuring resentment toward African-Americans suggests that racial attitudes were also a contributing factor.

An important question here is to what extent differences between the social characteristics and political attitudes of Tea Party supporters and nonsupporters can be explained simply by the fact that Tea Party support-ers were overwhelmingly Republicans. In order to answer this question, we need to know whether Republicans who supported the Tea Party dif-fered from those who did not. Table 6.4 compares the social characteris-tics and political attitudes of these two types of Republicans.

The results displayed in Table 6.4 indicate that Republican sup-porters of the Tea Party movement differed in a number of important respects from other Republicans, sometimes fairly dramatically. In terms of social characteristics, the most striking differences involved gender, age, and religiosity. Tea Party Republicans were disproportionately male, somewhat older, and much more religious than other Republicans. More

TABLE 6.4

Social Characteristics and Political Attitudes of Republican Tea Party Supporters versus Other Republicans

	TEA PARTY SUPPORTERS (%)	OTHER REPUBLICANS (%)
SOCIAL CHARACTERISTICS AND ATTITUDES		
AGE > 44	70	59
WHITE	86	89
MALE	66	48
MARRIED	62	63
INCOME $75,000+	32	27
COLLEGE GRAD	28	32
BORN AGAIN/EVANGELICAL	52	38
WEEKLY CHURCHGOER	52	42
BELIEVE BIBLE, ACTUAL WORD OF GOD	47	34
GUN OWNER	44	42
POLITICAL AND RACIAL ATTITUDES		
STRONG REPUBLICAN IDEOLOGY	45	21
CONSERVATIVE IDEOLOGY	90	62
DISLIKE OBAMA	90	55
LIKE PALIN	82	38
BIRTHER	46	37
OPPOSE ENDING "DON'T ASK, DON'T TELL"	71	44
OPPOSE CLEAN ENERGY	81	32
OPPOSE HEALTH CARE REFORM	88	58
OPPOSE STEM CELL RESEARCH	71	41
OPPOSE ECONOMIC STIMULUS	91	62
DISAGREE BLACKS ARE VICTIMS	74	54
DISAGREE BLACKS GOTTEN LESS	77	58
AGREE BLACKS NEED TO TRY HARDER	65	42
AGREE NO FAVORS FOR BLACKS	82	65

Source: ANES Evaluations of Government and Society Survey, October 2010

importantly, there were substantial differences between the political atti-tudes of supporters and nonsupporters. Compared with other Republicans, Tea Party supporters were much more likely to identify strongly with the GOP, to describe their political views as conservative, to dislike Barack Obama, to like Sarah Palin, to question whether Obama was born in the United States, and to oppose a variety of Obama Administration policy initiatives. Tea Party supporters were not just Republicans; they were super-Republicans.

The data in Table 6.4 show that the characteristics and attitudes of Tea Party supporters cannot be explained simply by their Republican loyalties. Tea Party supporters clearly stood out from other Republicans in terms of some of their characteristics and especially in terms of their polit-ical outlook. In addition, Tea Party supporters scored substantially higher on the racial resentment items than other Republicans. These findings raise the question of how much each of these factors contributed to support for the Tea Party movement.

EXPLAINING TEA PARTY SUPPORT: A MULTIVARIATE ANALYSIS

In order to determine the relative contributions of party identification, ideological conservatism, racial resentment, and demographic characteris-tics to support for the Tea Party movement among the public, I conducted a logistic regression analysis of Tea Party support among white respon-dents. I excluded nonwhites from the analysis because there were very few nonwhite supporters of the Tea Party movement in the sample. However, including nonwhites has almost no impact on the results.

The independent variables in this analysis are a nine-item ideology scale[10] combining ideological identification with opinions on eight policy issues (repeal of "don't ask don't tell," health care reform, expansion of the State Children's Health Insurance Program, the economic stimulus

---

[10]This scale appears to have a high level of internal reliability, as indicated by a Cronbach's alpha score of .92.

program, federal funding of stem cell research, federal funding of clean energy research and development, financial reform, and raising taxes on upper income households), the seven-point party identification scale, the four-item racial resentment scale, the Obama like-dislike scale, and five social characteristics—age, gender, education, family income, and frequency of church attendance. The results are displayed in Table 6.5.

The independent variables included in the analysis do a very good job of predicting support for the Tea Party movement, with an overall accuracy rate of 85 percent. In order to compare the effects of these independent variables, I calculated the change in the probability of supporting the Tea Party associated with an increase of one standard deviation above the mean on each independent variable with all other independent variables set at their means. For example, an increase of one standard deviation above the mean on the ideology scale is estimated to produce an increase of almost 19 percentage points in Tea Party support.

The results in Table 6.5 show that ideology was by far the strongest predictor of Tea Party support. This can be seen by comparing the change

TABLE 6.5
Logistic Regression Analysis of Tea Party Support among Whites

INDEPENDENT VARIABLE	LOGIT COEFFICIENT	STANDARD ERROR	SIGNIFICANCE	CHANGE IN PROBABILITY
AGE	.141	.060	.01	+.027
FEMALE	−.511	.191	.01	−.024
EDUCATION	.073	.055	.10	+.016
INCOME	−.033	.025	.10	−.013
CHURCH ATTENDANCE	−.011	.057	n.s.	−.000
PARTY IDENTIFICATION	−.188	.064	.01	−.034
CONSERVATISM	.354	.041	.001	+.187
DISLIKE OF OBAMA	.227	.071	.001	+.063
RACIAL RESENTMENT	.155	.034	.001	+.118
CONSTANT	−6.137			

Source: ANES Evaluations of Government and Society Survey, October 2010
Note: Significance levels based on one-tailed test.

in the probability of supporting the Tea Party associated with a change of one unit on each independent variable. In addition to conservatism, however, both racial resentment and dislike for Barack Obama had significant effects on support for the Tea Party. These two variables had much stronger effects than party identification. Racial resentment had a somewhat stronger effect than dislike for Obama. Moreover, dislike for Obama was itself very strongly related to racial resentment, with a correlation of .46. Finally, two social background characteristics, age and gender, had significant effects on Tea Party support, with older respondents and men more likely to support the Tea Party. However, these effects were much smaller than those for ideology, racial resentment, and dislike of Obama. These results clearly show that the rise of the Tea Party movement was a direct result of the growing racial and ideological polarization of the American electorate. The Tea Party drew its support very disproportionately from Republican identifiers who were white, conservative, and very upset about the presence of a black man in the White House—a black man whose supporters looked very different from themselves.

TEA PARTY SUPPORT AND POLITICAL ACTIVISM

We have seen thus far that Tea Party supporters differed from other Republicans in their demographic characteristics and especially in their political attitudes. However, the significance of these differences depends on the relative levels of political activism of these two types of Republicans. We will see that the impact of the Tea Party movement on the Republican Party was accentuated by the fact that Tea Party supporters were much more politically active than other Republicans.

Table 6.6 displays data comparing Republicans who supported the Tea Party movement with those who did not support the movement on several measures of political activism. In every case, Tea Party supporters were substantially more active than nonsupporters. Tea Party supporters were much more likely than nonsupporters to be registered to vote and to report that within the past year they had contacted a public official to express an opinion on an issue, given

TABLE 6.6

Political Activities of Republican Tea Party Supporters versus Other Republicans

ACTIVITY	TEA PARTY SUPPORTERS (%)	OTHER REPUBLICANS (%)
REGISTERED TO VOTE	92	75
CONTACTED PUBLIC OFFICIAL	44	20
GIVEN MONEY TO CAMPAIGN	22	9
ATTENDED RALLY/MEETING	24	7
DISPLAYED SIGN/BUMPER STICKER	25	11

Source: ANES Evaluations of Government and Society Survey, October 2010

money to a candidate or party, attended a political meeting or rally, and displayed a yard sign or bumper sticker.

The relatively high levels of activism of Republicans supporting the Tea Party movement mean that the composition of various groups of GOP activists is skewed toward supporters of the movement. Tea Party supporters made up 45 percent of all Republican identifiers but they made up 63 percent of Republicans who reported contacting an elected official, 65 percent of Republicans who reported giving money to a party or candidate, and 73 percent of Republicans who reported attending a political rally or meeting. Thus, the impact of the Tea Party movement on the Republican Party is magnified by the greater political activism of its supporters compared with other rank-and-file Republicans. Looking ahead to the 2012 presidential and congressional primaries, this finding suggests that Tea Party supporters are very likely to comprise a disproportionate share— and in many states and congressional districts an outright majority—of voters in Republican primaries.

CHAPTER SUMMARY

The Tea Party movement did not suddenly emerge on the American political scene in 2009 in response to the liberal policy agenda set forth by President Obama and the Democratic Congress. Rather, it was the natural outgrowth of the growing conservatism and activism of the Republican electoral base during the preceding decades. By 2009, a large cadre of very conservative and politically engaged Republicans was available for mobilization by conservative organizations and media outlets. But the Tea Party movement was not just a product of the growing polarization of the American electorate—it has also contributed to that polarization. Because Tea Party supporters are both more conservative and more active than other Republicans, they have helped to shift the party further to the right by influencing the selection of candidates in Republican primaries and by pressuring Republican candidates and elected officials to adopt conservative positions on a wide range of issues, positions that are in many cases far to the right of those of the average voter.

According to the October 2010 wave of the EGSS, although only a small fraction of voting-age Americans have ever participated in a Tea Party rally or contributed money to a Tea Party organization, almost a quarter of the American public considered themselves to be supporters of the Tea Party movement. These Tea Party supporters were overwhelmingly white, disproportionately male, somewhat older, and a good deal more religious than the overall electorate—all characteristics also present among active Republican identifiers. But by far the most striking differences between Tea Party supporters and the overall public involved their political beliefs.

Tea Party supporters overwhelmingly identified with the Republican Party, and they were much more conservative than the overall public and even other Republicans on a wide range of issues, including social issues as well as economic issues. Moreover, Tea Party supporters displayed high levels of racial resentment and held very negative opinions about President Obama compared with the rest of the public and even other Republicans. In a multivariate analysis, racial resentment and dislike of Barack Obama, along with conservatism, emerged as the most important factors contributing to support for the Tea Party movement.

These findings suggest that the Tea Party movement is not likely to fade away any time in the near future. Even without large-scale Tea Party rallies and protests, as long as Barack Obama remains in the White House, Tea Party supporters are likely to remain highly motivated to oppose his policy agenda and remove him from the White House. And given the fact that they make up almost half of Republican identifiers and a much larger proportion of active Republicans, Tea Party supporters appear to have the potential to strongly influence Republican congressional and presidential primaries in 2012. Any serious Republican presidential contender will have to find a way to appeal to Tea Party supporters. The risk, of course, is that this may make it very difficult for the eventual Republican nominee to appeal to moderate swing voters in the general election.

CHAPTER 7

Polarization Continues: The 2012 Elections and Beyond

The single most important thing we want to achieve is for President Obama to be a one-term president.

—Senate Minority Leader Mitch McConnell (R-KY), interview with the *National Journal*, October 23, 2010

On one level, Mitch McConnell's statement that his top priority as the leader of the Republican Party in the U.S. Senate was defeating Barack Obama in 2012 was rather surprising. At a time when the nation was facing serious challenges at home and abroad, one might expect someone in a key leadership position to have mentioned passing some major piece of legislation in the next two years as his top objective. And indeed, McConnell's statement was widely criticized by Democratic leaders and liberal pundits.[1] But on another level, McConnell's statement was not surprising at all. It simply reflected his belief—a belief that was probably shared by almost all Republican members of Congress—that given the deep ideological divide between congressional Republicans and

---

[1]See, for example, Steve Benen, "The Value of McConnell's Occasional Candor," *Washington Monthly*, Political Animal blog (October 25, 2010): http://www.washingtonmonthly.com/archives/individual/2010_10/026298.php.

the president, none of his party's policy goals could be accomplished as long as Barack Obama was in the White House.

Two years after Mitch McConnell made his controversial comments to the *National Journal*, the United States is approaching the 2012 presidential and congressional elections with a deeply divided government and a deeply divided citizenry. The 2010 midterm elections ended a rare two-year period of unified Democratic control of the presidency and both chambers of Congress—a period during which Democrats enacted some major pieces of legislation but frequently struggled to obtain the sixty votes needed to overcome Republican filibusters in the Senate. With a greatly diminished Democratic majority in the Senate and the largest Republican majority in the House of Representatives since the 1940s, President Obama and congressional Democrats found themselves on the defensive as energized Republicans sought to repeal much of the legislative handiwork of the previous two years while using the threats of a government shutdown and a default on the national debt to extract concessions from Democrats.[2]

The major result of the 2010 midterm election, though, was legislative gridlock. Neither Democrats nor Republicans had the votes to achieve their own legislative objectives. For the most part, Democrats did not even try to advance a legislative agenda in the Senate, knowing that anything they supported would face a near-certain Republican filibuster and would have no chance of passing in the House. House Republicans did move forward with bills repealing the Democratic health care law, defunding Planned Parenthood, and requiring a balanced federal budget. But the House GOP's conservative agenda never had any chance of becoming law as long as Democrats controlled the Senate and President Obama wielded the veto pen.

Divided government has been a fairly common occurrence in the United States since the end of World War II. And in the past it has not always led to gridlock. In fact, a study by political scientist David Mayhew concluded that just as much major legislation had been enacted during

---

[2]See Andrew Leonard, "The Next Horrible Budget Showdown," *Salon.com* (August 3, 2011): http://www.salon.com/technology/how_the_world_works/2011/08/03/the_next_horrible_budget_showdown.

periods of divided government as during periods of unified party control.[3] However, most of the data for Mayhew's study came from before the recent era of intense partisan polarization. It is highly questionable whether his conclusions would apply to divided government in the twenty-first century. Under divided government, major legislation can come about only through bipartisan compromise. But bipartisan compromise was much easier when there were large numbers of moderate Democrats and Republicans in the House and Senate. During the '50s, '60s, and '70s, reaching across the aisle did not involve reaching very far—moderate members of each party could easily find moderate members of the opposing party to work with.

Today, there are very few moderate Democrats and almost no moderate Republicans left in either the House or the Senate.[4] In fact, the Republican majority in the 112th House may be the most conservative group of Republicans in that body since at least the end of World War II.[5] The 2010 midterm election eliminated a large proportion of the moderate Democrats in the House since they had mainly represented Republican-leaning and swing districts. But few of the Republicans who replaced those moderate Democrats were themselves moderates. In fact, many of the new House Republicans were elected with the support of the Tea Party movement, and their voting records in the 112th Congress have reflected their Tea Party origins. As a result, the ideological divide between the parties in the House of Representatives may well be the deepest in the past century, and the divide in the Senate is only slightly smaller. Under these circumstances, the chances of any sort of bipartisan compromise on major policy issues are very poor. Until one side or the other achieves control of the presidency and both houses of Congress, with at least sixty votes to cut off filibusters in the Senate, the gridlock in Washington is likely to continue.

---

[3]David R. Mayhew, *Divided We Govern: Party Control, Lawmaking and Investigations, 1946–1990* (New Haven: Yale University Press, 1991). Mayhew's conclusions have not gone unchallenged, however. See Sarah Binder, "The Dynamics of Legislative Gridlock, 1947–96," *American Political Science Review* 93 (1999): 519–33.

[4]For evidence on the decline of moderates in Congress, see Keith T. Poole and Howard Rosenthal, *Ideology and Congress* (New Brunswick, NJ: Transaction Press, 2007).

[5]Alan I. Abramowitz, "Expect Confrontation, Not Compromise," *PS: Political Science and Politics* 44 (2011): 293–95.

THE OUTLOOK FOR 2012: THE REPUBLICAN PRESIDENTIAL NOMINATION

With control of both chambers of Congress and the presidency hanging in the balance and the policy divide between the parties as deep as it has ever been, the stakes for the nation in 2012 are clearly enormous. And nowhere are the stakes greater, of course, than in the battle for the White House. In 2008, Barack Obama became the nation's first African-American president and the first nonsouthern Democrat to win the White House since John F. Kennedy. Obama won the presidential election by a decisive margin by promising to use the power of the federal government to create jobs, expand access to health care, protect the environment, and strengthen regulation of financial institutions. In 2012, after achieving mixed results in all of these areas, the president is likely to face a Republican nominee committed to reversing all of these policies and to moving the country in a far more conservative direction on social as well as economic issues.

No matter who wins the Republican presidential nomination in 2012, the general election is certain to provide voters with a clear ideological choice. While President Obama has disappointed some liberal groups and commentators by not being a more aggressive advocate for liberal policies during his time in the White House, and especially since the Republican gains in the 2010 midterm elections, there is no doubt that he will run in 2012 as a progressive Democrat, vigorously defending the 2010 health care reform law and supporting a woman's right to choose, increased federal investments in education, scientific research and clean energy, increased spending on infrastructure repair and construction projects, federal aid to local school districts to hire additional teachers, and higher taxes on upper income Americans to pay for these programs.[6] And there is no doubt that the president's Republican challenger will be a strong conservative who

---

[6]Many of these proposals were incorporated in the American Jobs Act, which was unveiled by the President Obama in September of 2011. The American Jobs Act was widely interpreted by political commentators as less of a serious legislative initiative, since most of the bill's specific proposals were given little or no chance of passage in the Republican-controlled House, than an attempt by the president to appeal to the Democratic base in preparation for the 2012 presidential campaign. See David Jackson, "Obama's Jobs Bill: Plan or Campaign Plank?" *USA Today* (October 7, 2011): http://content.usatoday.com/communities/theoval/post/2011/10/obamas-jobs-bill-plan-or-campaign-plank/1.

supports repeal of the 2010 health care reform law, greater restrictions on access to abortion, and substantial cuts in federal spending on domestic social programs and opposes any increases in federal taxes.

In 2008, John McCain won the Republican presidential nomination even though his candidacy aroused little enthusiasm among the party's conservative base. McCain's long record of public service, his status as a war hero, and the fact that the conservative vote was split among several candidates enabled him to win many GOP primaries with less than 50 percent of the vote.[7] In the crucial early primary in South Carolina, for example, McCain finished first with only 33 percent of the vote. According to the data from the South Carolina exit poll, conservatives made up 69 percent of Republican primary voters and McCain won only 26 percent of the conservative vote. However, the remainder of the conservative vote was split three ways, with Mike Huckabee taking 35 percent, Fred Thompson 19 percent, and Mitt Romney 16 percent. In South Carolina and many other states, Republican winner-take-all rules allowed McCain to win almost all of the national convention delegates with a plurality of the vote.

John McCain did not run as a moderate in the 2008 Republican primaries, but he had a moderate reputation and a history of cooperating with Democrats. That reputation and history almost cost him the nomination. If Fred Thompson had not stayed in the race until after the South Carolina primary, Mike Huckabee would almost certainly have finished first in the Palmetto State and the outcome of the nomination might have been different.

In 2012, it is unlikely that a candidate with a relatively moderate reputation or a history of cooperating with Democrats will again win the Republican presidential nomination. In fact, almost all of the candidates in the early going have been working hard to shore up their conservative credentials by attacking President Obama, calling for repeal of the health care reform law and endorsing a balanced budget amendment to the U.S. Constitution.[8]

---

[7]For an in-depth account of the 2008 Republican nomination race, see John Heilemann and Mark Halperin, *Game Change: Obama and the Clintons, McCain and Palin and the Race of a Lifetime* (New York: HarperCollins, 2010).

[8]See Dick Pohlman, "The American Debate: Republicans Are Running Right, Maybe Right Off the Map," *Philadelphia Inquirer*, philly.com (August 28, 2011): http://articles.philly.com/2011-08-28/news/29938476_1_independent-voters-president-obama-general-election.

Of course, some candidates, like Mitt Romney, who was generally viewed as a moderate Republican during his years as governor of Massachusetts, have had to work harder than others.

By early December of 2011, only a few weeks before the critical early contests in Iowa, New Hampshire, and South Carolina, the race for the GOP nomination appeared to have narrowed down to two major candidates—Romney and former House speaker Newt Gingrich—and several minor candidates, including Texas congressman Ron Paul, former Utah governor and ambassador to China Jon Huntsman, former Pennsylvania senator Rick Santorum, and Minnesota congressperson Michele Bachmann. While Romney had been portrayed by most political observers as the early favorite for the nomination, Gingrich was able to take the lead in the national polls as well as in Iowa and South Carolina following the failures of several other conservative challengers to Romney, including Bachmann, Perry, and business executive and right-wing talk show host Herman Cain, whose candidacy collapsed following allegations of sexual harassment and extramarital affairs. Cain's collapse and subsequent withdrawal from the race clearly benefited Gingrich, whose polling numbers rose dramatically in late November and early December despite widespread concerns about his character and electability on the part of many Republican officeholders and strategists.

It is difficult to predict the course of a presidential nomination race given the importance of the early contests and the potential impact of campaign gaffes and unforeseen events, but Herman Cain's rapid rise in the polls and his subsequent replacement by Newt Gingrich can both be seen as reflecting the desire of many conservative Republican voters to find an alternative to Mitt Romney, who was seen as too moderate or unreliable. For example, in a December 1–5 Gallup Poll, Gingrich led Romney among all Republicans and Republican-leaning independents by 37 percent to 22 percent. Gingrich's overall lead was due to his big advantage among conservatives, who comprised a majority of Republican identifiers and leaners. Among moderates and liberals, Gingrich led Romney by only 2 percentage points, 28 percent to 26 percent, but among conservatives, Gingrich led Romney by 21 percentage points, 41 percent to 20 percent.

Gingrich was also doing very well among several other key Republican voter groups: he led Romney by 42 percent to 15 percent among southerners and by 43 to 22 percent among men. Perhaps most importantly, Gingrich led Romney by 47 to 17 percent among Republicans and Republican-leaning independents who described themselves as Tea Party supporters, a group that comprised a majority of all Republican voters and one whose members were generally more motivated to turn out in GOP primaries and caucuses than other Republicans.

These results suggest that Mitt Romney is likely to continue experiencing difficulty in appealing to conservatives and Tea Party supporters once actual voting begins. Romney's best hope of winning the Republican nomination might be that in 2012, as in 2008, the conservative vote ends up being split among several candidates. According to the revised Republican rules, in 2012, unlike 2008, no winner-take-all contests will be permitted until April. However, once this deadline passes, a candidate like Romney might be able to pile up a large lead in delegates and quickly lock up the nomination if he can finish first in big state primaries with large blocs of delegates. This was the strategy that was used successfully by John McCain in 2008, but the rise of Newt Gingrich as the leading conservative candidate by early December appeared to make this path to the nomination much more difficult for Mitt Romney.

The advantages enjoyed by conservative candidates in Republican primaries as well as the potential problems that such candidates can experience in a general election are both underscored by the evidence in Table 7.1. This table compares the characteristics and political attitudes of Republican presidential primary voters with the characteristics and attitudes of general election voters in 2008 based on data from the American National Election Study (ANES). The results show that Republican primary voters were older and more religious than general election voters. But the biggest differences between Republican primary voters and general election voters involved their political beliefs.

Almost 90 percent of GOP primary voters were conservatives and almost two-thirds were strong conservatives, placing themselves at either six or seven on the ANES seven-point ideology scale. And the conservative label was consistent with the positions taken by these voters on social and

TABLE 7.1

Characteristics and Political Attitudes of 2008 Republican Presidential Primary Voters versus All General Election Voters

	REPUBLICAN PRIMARY VOTERS (%)	ALL GENERAL ELECTION VOTERS (%)
WHITE	94	76
UNDER AGE 30	10	17
65 OR OLDER	30	20
BORN AGAIN, EVANGELICAL	62	40
WEEKLY CHURCHGOER	59	37
CONSERVATIVE	86	44
STRONG CONSERVATIVE	64	28
PRO-LIFE ON ABORTION	59	39
OPPOSE GAY ADOPTION	68	48
OPPOSE UNIVERSAL HEALTH CARE	77	40

Source: 2008 American National Election Study

economic issues. The large majority of Republican primary voters were pro-life on abortion, opposed to allowing gay couples to adopt children, and opposed to a government-sponsored universal health care plan—all positions that put them at odds with a majority of general election voters. And while these data are based on Republican primary voters in 2008, in the aftermath of the Tea Party movement one might expect Republican primary voters to be even more conservative in 2012.

THE OUTLOOK FOR 2012:
THE PRESIDENTIAL ELECTION

Every presidential election is largely a referendum on the performance of the incumbent president and this is especially true when the incumbent is on the ballot.[9] Regardless of who wins the Republican nomination, the

---

[9]For all fifteen presidential elections since World War II for which the data are available, the correlation between the incumbent president's net approval rating in the Gallup Poll at the time of the election and the incumbent party's share of the major party vote is a very strong .86. For the nine elections in which the incumbent was on the ballot, the correlation is an even stronger .93.

outcome of the 2012 presidential election will hinge primarily on how voters feel about President Obama. Almost from the beginning of his presidency, Americans have been deeply divided in their views about the president and there is no reason to think that is going to change before November of 2012. The divisions that were present in the 2008 electorate are almost certain to be present in the 2012 electorate. In fact, those divisions may be even deeper after four years of intense partisan conflict over Mr. Obama's policies and performance.

During the 2008 campaign, some political observers expressed the hope that a new president would have an opportunity to bridge the deep partisan divide that had developed in Washington and in the country during the eight years of George W. Bush's administration. Indeed, during the campaign, Barack Obama regularly talked about wanting to bring Americans together and change the way Washington works. But despite the president's frequent criticism of politics-as-usual and his oft-stated desire to work with Republicans to find solutions to the nation's problems, the partisan divide in Washington and the country remained as deep as ever.

The data in Figure 7.1 (see Chapter 7 color insert) from the ANES Evaluations of Government and Society Survey (EGSS) show that in the fall of 2010, less than two years into his presidency, opinions about Mr. Obama were sharply divided, with the large majority of Democrats rating him "very favorably," the large majority of Republicans rating him "very unfavorably," and very few Americans in the middle. On a zero-to-ten scale with zero the most negative rating and ten the most positive rating, only 18 percent of registered voters placed the president within one unit of the center of the scale, at four, five, or six. Sixty-three percent of Democrats gave Mr. Obama a rating of eight or higher while 63 percent of Republicans gave him a rating of two or lower.

With regard to Barack Obama, in the fall of 2010, Americans were closely divided as well as deeply divided. On our zero-to-ten scale, 47 percent of registered voters in the EGSS gave the president a positive rating (six to ten) while 46 percent gave him a negative rating (zero to four). Only 7 percent of registered voters gave the president a neutral rating (five). The results displayed in Table 7.2 show that the divisions within the

TABLE 7.2
Ratings of President Obama in 2010 by Voter Groups

	POSITIVE (%)	NEUTRAL (%)	NEGATIVE (%)
ALL REGISTERED VOTERS	47	7	46
WHITES	40	8	52
LATINOS	61	11	28
BLACKS	91	2	8
WHITES			
LIBERAL	82	3	15
MODERATE	48	15	36
CONSERVATIVE	12	7	80
BORN AGAIN, EVANGELICAL	21	6	73
OTHER	48	9	43
GUN OWNER	27	8	65
NOT GUN OWNER	49	8	43
UNION MEMBER	39	5	56
NOT UNION MEMBER	40	9	51
INCOME			
UNDER $50,000	41	9	50
$50,000–$74,999	42	6	52
$75,000–$99,999	35	7	58
$100,000+	42	8	50
HIGH SCHOOL	36	10	53
SOME COLLEGE	36	7	57
GRAD COLLEGE	48	7	45

Source: ANES Evaluations of Government and Society Survey, 2010

electorate in 2010 were very similar to the divisions within the electorate in 2008. There was, for example, a very deep racial divide in opinions of the president, with 91 percent of African-American voters and 61 percent of Latino voters giving Mr. Obama a positive rating compared with only 40 percent of white voters. The fifty-one-percentage-point favorability gap between whites and blacks was almost identical to the gap between whites and blacks in support for Mr. Obama in the 2008 election.

The data in Table 7.2 show that, in addition to a deep racial divide, white voters in 2010 were themselves sharply divided in their opinions of the president based on their ideological and cultural orientations. Fully 82 percent of liberal whites had a positive opinion of the president compared with 48 percent of moderate whites and 12 percent of conservative whites. Only 21 percent of whites who identified themselves as born-again or evangelical Christians had a positive opinion of Mr. Obama compared with 48 percent of other whites. Similarly, only 27 percent of whites who were gun owners had a positive opinion of the president compared with 49 percent of whites who were not gun owners.

In contrast to the large differences based on ideological and cultural orientations, differences in opinions of the president based on social class and union membership were relatively small and not always in the expected direction. The data in Table 7.2 show that lower-income whites were not more favorably inclined toward Mr. Obama than upper-income whites, white union members were no more positive in their evaluations than whites who were not union members, and white college graduates were actually more positive in their evaluations of the president than whites with only a high school education or some college.

Taken together, the results in Table 7.2 suggest that regardless of who wins the Republican nomination for president, the electoral coalitions supporting the parties in 2012 will be very similar to the electoral coalitions that supported the parties in 2008: the deep racial, ideological, and cultural divisions that were present in the 2008 electorate are almost certain to be present in the 2012 electorate. Nonwhites and white liberals will again make up the large majority of Democratic voters while conservative whites will again make up the large majority of Republican voters.

Of course, the outcome of the presidential election is based on electoral votes, not popular votes. With a total of 538 electoral votes at stake, and every state except Maine and Nebraska awarding all of its votes to the candidate receiving the most popular votes in the state, candidates focus their attention on the battleground states, where the outcome is in doubt. But just as the racial, ideological, and cultural divides within the electorate have been growing, so has the geographic divide. As we saw in Chapter 5, the number of states and electoral votes that are up for grabs has been shrinking over time while the number of states and electoral votes that are solidly in the Democratic camp or solidly in the Republican camp has been growing. In 2008, only six states were decided by a margin of less than 5 percentage points while twenty-six states and the District of Columbia were decided by a margin of at least 15 percentage points.

The geographic divide in 2012 will almost certainly be very similar to the geographic divide in the last three presidential elections. Based on the results of those elections, we can classify all fifty states and the District of Columbia into five categories according to their likelihood of supporting the Democratic or Republican candidate. The results are displayed in Table 7.3. Strongly Democratic states voted for the Democratic candidate by at least 5 percentage points in all three elections while strongly Republican states voted for the Republican candidate by at least 5 percentage points in all three elections. Unless something happens to produce a landslide or near-landslide margin in the national popular vote—a result that seems rather unlikely—all of these thirty-three states, and of course the District of Columbia, can be expected to end up supporting the same party again in 2012 in most if not all cases by a wide margin. That would give President Obama 179 electoral votes and his Republican challenger 166 electoral votes.

Another ten states (along with one congressional district in Nebraska—one of only two states that allows its electoral votes to be split) appear to lean toward one party or the other. Some of them, like Michigan and Pennsylvania, have supported the same party in all three elections but sometimes by only a narrow margin. Others, like Indiana and North Carolina, have supported candidates from both parties but have given much bigger margins to one party than the other—in this case the Republican Party. If the national popular vote is close, within 2 or 3 percentage points one way or the other, these states will most likely support the party they lean toward. Combined with the electoral votes of the strongly Democratic and strongly Republican states, that would give President Obama 247 electoral votes and his Republican challenger

TABLE 7.3
2012 Electoral College Outlook

STRONGLY DEMOCRATIC (179)	LEAN DEMOCRATIC (68)	TOSSUP (85)	LEAN REPUBLICAN (40)	STRONGLY REPUBLICAN (166)
California (55)	Michigan (16)	Colorado (9)	Indiana (11)	Alabama (9)
Connecticut (7)	Minnesota (10)	Florida (29)	Missouri (10)	Alaska (3)
Delaware (3)	New Mexico (5)	Iowa (6)	Montana (3)	Arizona (11)
D.C. (3)	Oregon (7)	Nevada (6)	North Carolina (15)	Arkansas (6)
Hawaii (4)	Pennsylvania (20)	North Hampshire (4)	Nebraska (1)	Georgia (16)
Illinois (20)	Wisconsin (10)	Ohio (18)		Idaho (4)
Maine (4)		Virginia (13)		Kansas (6)
Maryland (10)				Kentucky (8)
Massachusetts (11)				Louisiana (8)
New Jersey (14)				Mississippi (6)
New York (29)				Nebraska (4)
Rhode Island (4)				North Dakota (3)
Vermont (3)				Oklahoma (7)
Washington (12)				South Carolina (9)
				South Dakota (3)
				Tennessee (11)
				Texas (38)
				Utah (6)
				West Virginia (5)
				Wyoming (3)

Source: Data compiled by author

206 electoral votes. In that case, the outcome in the Electoral College will probably come down to seven toss-up states, with a total of eighty-five electoral votes—Colorado, Florida, Iowa, Nevada, New Hampshire, Ohio, and Virginia. President Obama would need to pick up at least twenty-three electoral votes from these states while his Republican challenger would need to pick up at least sixty-four. Lucky voters in those states can expect to see the presidential candidates in their states on a regular basis and to be bombarded by television ads, phone calls, and mailings during the final days of the campaign.

THE OUTLOOK FOR 2012: THE HOUSE OF REPRESENTATIVES

In addition to the president, voters will be choosing all 435 members of the House of Representatives and 33 members of the Senate in 2012. And control of both chambers could be up for grabs. In the 2010 midterm elections, Republicans gained a remarkable sixty-two seats in the House of Representatives, more than reversing the losses that they had suffered in 2006 and 2008 and giving them their largest majority in more than sixty years. They accomplished this stunning feat despite the fact that, as we saw in Chapter 5, there are far fewer competitive districts and far more safe districts in the House than at any time since at least the 1970s.

Going into the 2012 election, Republicans hold 242 House seats while Democrats hold 193. That means Democrats would have to pick up twenty-five seats to regain control of the House in the next Congress. It's a tall order, but two of the last three elections have seen even larger swings in House seats. In 2006, Democrats gained thirty seats to take control of the House for the first time since the 1994 election, and in 2010, as we know, Republicans gained sixty-two seats to take back the House. So a twenty-five-seat swing is not out of the question. But based on the numbers of safe and competitive districts currently held by each party, Democrats would have to pick up those twenty-five seats in the small minority of House districts that are likely to be in play in 2012.

TABLE 7.4
U.S. House Seats in 112th Congress

TYPE OF DISTRICT	SEATS CURRENTLY HELD BY		
	REPUBLICAN	DEMOCRAT	TOTAL
SAFE DEMOCRATIC	0	112	112
STRONGLY DEMOCRATIC	2	42	44
LEANS DEMOCRATIC	30	24	54
LEANS REPUBLICAN	55	4	59
STRONGLY REPUBLICAN	61	6	67
SAFE REPUBLICAN	94	5	99
TOTAL	242	193	435

Source: Data compiled by author

Table 7.4 displays the partisan composition of the House districts currently held by Democrats and Republicans, in the 112th Congress. House districts were classified based on the performance of the presidential candidates in each district in 2008 compared with their performance in the nation. A safe Democratic district was one in which Barack Obama's vote share was at least 10 percentage points higher than his national vote share while a safe Republican district was one in which John McCain's vote share was at least 10 percentage points higher than his national vote share. Similarly, a strongly Democratic district was one in which Obama's vote was between 5 and 10 percentage points higher than his national vote share while a strongly Republican district was one in which McCain's vote share was between 5 and 10 percentage points higher than his national vote share. Finally, a district was classified as leaning Democratic or leaning Republican if the vote share of the winning presidential candidate in the district was within 5 percentage points of his national vote share. Altogether, there were 211 safe Democratic or safe Republican districts, 111 strongly Democratic or strongly Republican districts, and 113 relatively competitive districts.

The data in Table 7.4 show that there was a very strong relationship between the partisan composition of House districts as measured by the results of the 2008 presidential election and the party of current House members in the 112th Congress. All 112 safe Democratic districts and 42 of 44 strongly Democratic districts are currently held by Democrats while 94 of 99 safe Republican districts and 61 of 67 strongly Republican districts are currently held by Republicans. This means that 309 out of 322 districts classified as safe or strongly favoring one party, or 96 percent, are currently held by a member of the dominant party in the district, with Democrats holding 165 of these seats and Republicans holding 157.

The main reason why Republicans have a big majority in the 112th House is that they hold a large majority of the seats in competitive districts—85 out of 113 to be exact. That represents a big change from the situation in the 111th House, when Republicans held only forty-four of those seats. So nearly two-thirds of the overall Republican gain of sixty-two seats occurred in the approximately one-quarter of House districts that are relatively competitive. All of the remaining Republican gains involved taking back almost all of the seats that Democrats were defending in solidly or safely Republican districts. Republicans made no gains, and in fact lost three seats, in safe or strongly Democratic districts.

As a result of the major gains made by Republicans in competitive House districts in 2010, Democrats should have a good chance of making at least modest gains in the 2012 House elections. Republicans will be defending not only fifty-five of fifty-nine seats in districts that lean Republican but also thirty of fifty-four seats in districts than lean Democratic. Even a modest swing in the national popular vote back toward Democrats—Republicans won about 53 percent of the major party vote in the 2010 House elections—would probably be put a number of these districts back in the Democratic column. Exactly how many would depend on the number of open seats that are available, the popularity of the Republican incumbents in these districts, the quality of the Democratic challengers, and one other factor that was not present in 2010—the results of redistricting, which could affect quite a few House races in 2012. Based on the results of earlier redistricting cycles, however, it is unlikely that redistricting will drastically affect either the balance of Democratic versus Republican districts or the numbers of safe versus competitive districts in the House.

Another factor that could come into play in a good many 2012 House races is the extraordinary conservatism of the Republican freshmen who were elected in 2010, in many cases with the support of the Tea Party movement. Even though many of these GOP freshmen represent marginal districts, including quite a few who represent marginally Democratic districts, the overwhelming majority of them have taken strongly conservative positions on a wide range of issues and voted in lock step with their party—something that one normally does not expect to see from freshmen members in marginal House districts. There has been little if any evidence of moderation among members of the Republican class of 2010, and that could make it more likely that they will attract strong, well-financed Democratic challengers and face difficult reelection battles in 2012.[10]

THE OUTLOOK FOR 2012: THE SENATE

Only thirty-three of the hundred seats in the U.S. Senate will be at stake in 2012 but control of the upper chamber clearly will be up for grabs. That is because Democrats currently hold a narrow 53-47 majority in the Senate, and twenty-three of the thirty-three seats that are up for election in 2012 are currently held by Democrats. Republicans would need to pick up only three or four seats to regain control of the Senate in the 113th Congress, depending on whether the vice president is a Democrat or a Republican. With twenty-three Democratic seats and only ten Republican seats up for election, a three- or four-seat gain is entirely possible.

Table 7.5 displays the partisan composition of the states currently represented by Democratic and Republican senators in the 112th Congress. States were classified based on the 2008 presidential vote, using the same system used to classify House districts, but the results were somewhat different. Based on this classification system, 72 percent of states were found to be either safe or strongly favoring one party—very close to the

---

[10]Ideological extremism and party-line voting are generally associated with poorer performance in general elections for congressional incumbents. See Brandice Canes-Wrone, David W. Brady, and John F. Coogan, "Out of Step, Out of Office: Electoral Accountability and House Members' Voting," *American Political Science Review* 96 (2002): 127–40.

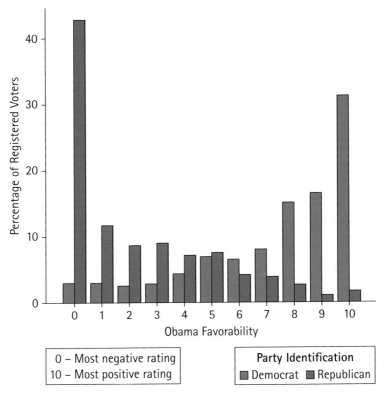

FIGURE 7.1
Ratings of President Obama by Party Identification in 2010

Percentage of Registered Voters

Obama Favorability

| 0 – Most negative rating |
| 10 – Most positive rating |

Party Identification
■ Democrat ■ Republican

Source: ANES Evaluations of Government and Society Survey
Note: Based on registered voters. Leaning independents included with party identifiers.

TABLE 7.5
U.S. Senate Seats in 112th Congress

TYPE OF STATE	SEATS CURRENTLY HELD BY		
	REPUBLICAN	DEMOCRAT	TOTAL
SAFE DEMOCRATIC	1	11	12
STRONGLY DEMOCRATIC	3	17	20
LEANS DEMOCRATIC	5	11	16
LEANS REPUBLICAN	6	6	12
STRONGLY REPUBLICAN	12	4	16
SAFE REPUBLICAN	20	4	24
TOTAL	47	53	100

Source: Data compiled by author

74 percent of House districts classified as safe or strongly favoring one party. In the Senate, however, there were twice as many safe Republican states as safe Democratic states while in the House safe Democratic seats outnumbered safe Republican seats. The difference between the two chambers reflects the overrepresentation of states with small populations in the Senate—states that disproportionately favor Republicans. Twelve of the twenty least populous states are classified as either safe or strongly Republican while only five are classified as safe or strongly Democratic. On the other hand, three of the five most populous states—California, New York, and Illinois—are strongly Democratic. California alone has a population larger than that of the twenty least populous states but those twenty states elect forty U.S. senators to California's two.

In the Senate, as in the House, there is a very strong relationship between the partisan orientation of the electorate as measured by the 2008 presidential vote and the party affiliation of the members. Of the seventy-two Senate seats from states classified as safe or strongly favoring one party, sixty, or 83 percent, are held by a senator from the dominant party. Democrats and Republicans each currently hold thirty-six of those seats. The reason why Democrats are still the majority party in the Senate despite the small-state Republican bias of the upper chamber is that they

TABLE 7.6
U.S. Senate Seats Up for Election in 2012

TYPE OF STATE	SEATS CURRENTLY HELD BY		
	REPUBLICAN	DEMOCRAT	TOTAL
SAFE DEMOCRATIC	1	5	6
STRONGLY DEMOCRATIC	1	7	8
LEANS DEMOCRATIC	1	4	5
LEANS REPUBLICAN	1	4	5
STRONGLY REPUBLICAN	3	2	5
SAFE REPUBLICAN	3	1	4
TOTAL	10	23	33

Source: Data compiled by author

hold seventeen of the twenty-eight seats from competitive states, including six of the twelve seats from states classified as leaning Republican. The question is how long they can continue to maintain that advantage.

To answer that question, we have to look more closely at the thirty-three Senate seats that are up for election in 2012. Table 7.6 displays the partisan orientations of the states currently represented by those twenty-three Democratic senators and ten Republican senators. The results indicate that Democrats currently hold seven seats in Republican states including three in safe or strongly Republican states while Republicans hold only three seats in Democratic states including two in safe or strongly Democratic states. This suggests that without taking into account factors such as the retirements, incumbent popularity, and challenger strength, Democrats would be expected to suffer some losses. In addition, however, by Labor Day of 2011, six Democratic incumbents had announced that they would not be running for reelection versus only two Republican incumbents. Moreover, both Republican retirements were in strongly Republican states, Arizona and Texas, lessening the chances of Democratic takeovers, while one Democratic retirement was in a safe Republican state, North Dakota, and one was in a swing state, Virginia. In addition, one Democratic incumbent in a strongly Republican state, Ben Nelson in Nebraska, appeared to be in serious danger and two other Democratic incumbents in Republican-leaning states, Jon Tester in Montana and Claire McCaskill in Missouri, are expected to face tough challenges.

Taking all of these factors into account, Democrats appeared likely to lose at least two or three seats and possibly as many as four or five. However, the Senate outlook in 2012 could again be affected by the efforts of the Tea Party movement. As in 2010, candidates aligned with the Tea Party movement could possibly challenge more moderate, establishment candidates in Republican primaries, including some Republican incumbents like Olympia Snowe in Maine and Richard Lugar in Indiana. To the extent that these Tea Party candidates are successful in winning GOP nominations in competitive or Democratic-leaning states, the prospects of the Republican Party making substantial gains in the Senate could well be reduced.

BEYOND 2012: GOVERNING IN
AN AGE OF POLARIZATION

Whether the 2012 elections result in unified Democratic control of Congress and the presidency, unified Republican control, or some type of split party control, the deep ideological divide between the two major parties will remain a major obstacle to any meaningful bipartisan compromise on major policy issues. Even under unified party control, it is almost certain that the minority party in the Senate will control considerably more than the forty-one votes needed to block legislation by using the filibuster. And neither party has shown any hesitation in recent years about using the filibuster along with holds and other delaying tactics to thwart the will of the majority. During 2009–2010, when Democrats controlled both chambers of Congress and the White House, Republicans routinely used filibusters and holds to block Democratic legislation and President Obama's nominees to the courts and key administrative positions.[11] There is little doubt that Senate Democrats

---

[11]See Josh Smith, "Majority Does Not Rule in Filibuster-Filled 111th Congress," *National Journal Daily* (December 17, 2010): http://www.nationaljournal.com/daily/majority-does-not-rule-in-filibuster-filled-111th-congress-20101216.

would use the same tactics to obstruct the will of a Republican president and Congress if they found themselves in the minority after the 2012 election.

The fundamental problem is that the American political system, based on the Madisonian principles of separation of powers and checks and balances, was not designed to work under conditions of intense partisan polarization. Political parties in their modern form did not exist at the time of the founding, of course. Indeed, the founders viewed parties as dangerous fomenters of conflict. But modern political parties quickly developed during the first half of the nineteenth century with the expansion of the franchise and the need to mobilize a mass electorate. Today, parties are generally considered essential for the effective functioning of representative democracy, providing a link between candidates and elected officials and the public and clarifying the choices for voters in elections.[12]

Within government, parties play a vital role in the American political system, by organizing the legislative process and helping to bridge the separation of powers by creating a bond of self-interest between the president and members of his party in the House and Senate.[13] For the bond of self-interest to work, however, the president and both chambers of Congress must be controlled by the same party. When that is not the case, and divided party control of the White House and at least one chamber has been much more common since World War II than previously, the result is either bipartisan compromise or gridlock and, as we have seen since the 2010 midterm election, which produced the most conservative House of Representatives in decades, the deeper the ideological divide between the parties, the greater the likelihood of gridlock.

There are two formulas for overcoming gridlock. One involves bipartisan compromise, which is the preferred solution of many editorial writers and pundits. They wonder why Democrats and Republicans cannot get together and move past their parties' entrenched positions to "do what is in the best interest of the country." The answer is that Democrats and

---

[12]See, for example, V. O. Key, Jr., *Public Opinion and American Democracy* (New York: Knopf, 1961). See also E. E. Schattschneider, *Party Government* (New York: Farrar and Rinehart, 1942).

[13]See George C. Edwards, *At the Margins: Presidential Leadership of Congress* (New Haven: Yale University Press, 1989).

Republicans today profoundly disagree on what is in the best interest of the country. In fact, their ideas about what should be done to address the nation's biggest problems are fundamentally incompatible. Democrats, for example, believe strongly that the best way to create jobs and grow the economy is to increase government spending in order to stimulate demand for goods and services while Republicans believe just as strongly that the best way to create jobs and grow the economy is to reduce government spending and regulation and cut taxes on corporations and upper-income Americans in order to increase incentives for investment in the private sector. And when it comes to cultural issues like abortion, the divide is even deeper. It is almost impossible to reconcile the view of most Democrats that women have a fundamental right to choose whether to continue a pregnancy and the view of most Republicans that abortion is immoral and should be banned or allowed only under extraordinary circumstances.

As long as these fundamental differences between Democrats and Republicans continue to exist—and there is little reason to expect them to disappear any time soon—bipartisan compromise is going to be very difficult. And simply urging an end to partisan infighting, as many pundits and editorial writers have done, is not going to accomplish anything. The diverging positions of Democratic and Republican elected officials and candidates reflect the diverging positions of those who put them in office.

A more plausible formula for overcoming gridlock under these circumstances is party government. Under party government, a system that exists in some countries with a parliamentary political system, the party that wins an election gets to carry out the policies it campaigned on until the next election, at which point the voters get to choose whether to keep that party in power or replace it with the opposition party.[14] But this system requires unified party control of the executive and legislative branches for a long enough time period to allow the majority party's policies to be implemented and work, a requirement that midterm elections frequently interfere with. And party government would also require an end to antimajoritarian rules like the Senate filibuster, which allow the

---

[14]E. E. Schattschneider, *Party Government* (New York: Farrar and Rinehart, 1942).

minority party to frustrate the will of the majority. Party government is a risky approach to policy making because it requires the minority party to accept the right of the majority party to implement its preferred policies no matter how much the minority party dislikes those policies. But the fact that the majority party is likely to find itself in the minority at some point in the near future can act as a check on abuses of power or ideological overreach. And in a polarized political system, the alternative to party government is not bipartisan compromise—it is continued gridlock.

Index